Guide

Attestation Engagements on Sustainability Information (Including Greenhouse Gas Emissions Information)

June 1, 2017

Copyright © 2017 by
American Institute of Certified Public Accountants, Inc.
New York, NY 10036-8775

All rights reserved. For information about the procedure for requesting permission to make copies of any part of this work, please e-mail copyright@aicpa.org with your request. Otherwise, requests should be written and mailed to the Permissions Department, AICPA, 220 Leigh Farm Road, Durham, NC 27707-8110.

1 2 3 4 5 6 7 8 9 0 AAP 1 9 8 7

ISBN 978-1-94549-862-6

Preface

About AICPA Guides

This AICPA guide has been developed by the AICPA Auditing Standards Board (ASB) Sustainability Task Force to assist practitioners in performing and reporting on their attestation engagements of entities' sustainability information.

The guide includes sections following the last chapter. These sections are entitled "Appendix." An appendix is included for informational purposes and has no authoritative status.

An AICPA guide containing attestation guidance is recognized as an interpretive publication as defined in AT-C section 105, *Concepts Common to All Attestation Engagements*.[1] Interpretive publications are recommendations on the application of Statements on Standards for Attestation Engagements (SSAEs) in specific circumstances, including engagements for entities in specialized industries. Interpretive publications are issued under the authority of the ASB. The members of the ASB have found the attestation guidance in this guide to be consistent with existing SSAEs.

A practitioner should be aware of and consider the guidance in this guide applicable to his or her attestation engagement. If the practitioner does not apply the attestation guidance included in an applicable AICPA guide, the practitioner should be prepared to explain how he or she complied with the SSAE provisions addressed by such attestation guidance.

Any attestation guidance in an appendix or exhibit (whether a chapter or back matter appendix or exhibit) though not authoritative, is considered an "other attestation publication." In applying such guidance, the practitioner should, exercising professional judgment, assess the relevance and appropriateness of such guidance to the circumstances of the engagement. Although the practitioner determines the relevance of other attestation guidance, such guidance in a guide appendix or exhibit has been reviewed by the AICPA Audit and Attest Standards staff and the practitioner may presume that it is appropriate.

The ASB is the designated senior committee of the AICPA authorized to speak for the AICPA on all matters related to attestation.

Purpose and Applicability

This guide has been prepared to assist practitioners engaged to perform an examination or review engagement of an entity's sustainability information and, accordingly, includes performance and reporting guidance on applying the clarified attestation standards to the subject matter of sustainability information.

This guide is applicable when the reporting entity is holding the subject matter out as sustainability information or makes an assertion that it is sustainability information. Examples of ways in which the reporting entity might hold out the subject matter as sustainability information include the following:

- Labeling the report containing the subject matter as a sustainability report, a corporate social responsibility report, an environmental, social, and governance report, or a similar title

---

[1] All AT-C sections cited in the preface can be found in AICPA *Professional Standards*.

- Labeling the presentation of information as a greenhouse gas (GHG) emissions schedule or statement

- Submitting the presentation in response to a third-party requirement for the submission of sustainability information (for example, to sustainability rating bodies)

- Labeling sections of a broader report, such as in a report submitted to a securities regulator (for example, in the "Management's Discussion and Analysis" section of an SEC Form 10-K), as sustainability, corporate social responsibility; or environmental, social and governance information

- Labeling the subject matter appearing on the entity's website as sustainability, corporate social responsibility, or environmental, social and governance information, or a similar title

- Citing a sustainability framework, including standards, regulations, and entity-specific criteria for sustainability information, as criteria for the preparation or presentation of the subject matter

Given the varied nature of the subject matter, the practitioner may need to exercise judgment in ascertaining whether the guide is applicable to the engagement.

A practitioner is required to comply with AT-C section 105 and either AT-C section 205, *Examination Engagements*, for examinations of sustainability information; or AT-C section 210, *Review Engagements*, for reviews of sustainability information. In some cases, this guide repeats or refers to requirements found in AT-C sections 105, 205, and 210 when describing those requirements in the context of an examination or review of sustainability information. Although not all the requirements in AT-C sections 105, 205, and 210 are repeated or referred to in this guide, the practitioner is responsible for complying with all the requirements in AT-C sections 105, 205, and 210, as applicable.

If the entity is engaging the practitioner to perform the examination or review of sustainability information for purposes of including the practitioner's report in an SEC filing, the practitioner should perform the engagement in accordance with AICPA attestation standards, as such an engagement as of the date of this guide is not within the jurisdiction of the PCAOB. The practitioner may, however, agree to perform the engagement in accordance with both AICPA attestation standards and other standards, such as the interim attestation standards of the PCAOB or the International Standards on Assurance Engagements of the International Auditing and Assurance Standards Board. In such situations, the practitioner is required to comply with AICPA attestation standards and any more stringent requirements included in such other standards.

Although this guide is not intended to provide guidance for agreed-upon procedures (AUP) engagements, AT-C section 215, *Agreed-Upon Procedures Engagements*, is applicable when a practitioner is performing an AUP engagement related to sustainability information, and certain definitional and background materials in this guide may be useful to the practitioner in performing AUP engagements on sustainability information.

This guide incorporates information regarding GHG emissions contained in AICPA Statement of Position 13-1, *Attest Engagements on Greenhouse Gas Emissions Information*, which has been superseded by this guide.

Recognition

AICPA Senior Committees
Auditing Standards Board (2016–2017)

Michael J. Santay, *Chair*
Gerry Boaz
Jay Brodish, Jr.
Dora Burzenski
Joseph S. Cascio
Lawrence M. Gill
Steven M. Glover
Daniel J. Hevia
Gaylen R. Hansen
Tracy W. Harding
Ilene Kassman
G. Alan Long
Richard Miller
Daniel D. Montgomery
Steven Morrision
Richard N. Reisig
Catherine M. Schweigel
Jere G. Shawver
Chad Singletary

Assurance Services Executive Committee (2016–2017)

Robert Dohrer, *Chair*
Bradley Ames
Christine M. Anderson
Brad Beasley
Nancy Bumgarner
Jim Burton
MaryGrace Davenport
Chris Halterman
Jennifer Haskell
Brad Muniz
Michael Ptasienski
Joanna Purtell
Miklos Vasarhelyi

The AICPA gratefully acknowledges those members of the AICPA ASB Sustainability Task Force who developed the guide: Dorsey Baskin, John DeRose, Marne Doman, Bryce Gibbs, Eric Hespenheide, Susan Jones, Fain McDaniel, Justin Neff, Paul Penler, D. Scott Showalter, Chris Smith, and the chair of the task force, Beth A. Schneider.

AICPA Staff

Charles E. Landes
Vice President
Professional Standards and Services

Amy Pawlicki
Vice President
Assurance and Advisory Innovation

Desiré Carroll
Senior Technical Manager
Assurance and Advisory Innovation
and
Staff Liaison to the AICPA ASB Sustainability Task Force

Guidance Considered in This Edition

This guide considers relevant guidance issued through June 1, 2017. In particular, this guide reflects SSAE No. 18, *Attestation Standards: Clarification and Recodification* (AICPA, *Professional Standards*).

This guide does not include all attestation requirements that may be applicable to the types of engagements covered by this guide. This guide is intended to be used in conjunction with all applicable sources of relevant guidance. In determining the applicability of recently issued guidance, the effective date of the guidance should also be considered.

Terms Used to Define Professional Requirements in This AICPA Guide

Any requirements described in this guide are normally referenced to the applicable standards or regulations from which they are derived. Generally, the terms used in this guide describing the professional requirements of the referenced standard setter (for example, the ASB) are the same as those used in the applicable standards or regulations (for example, "must" or "should").

Readers should refer to the applicable standards and regulations for more information on the requirements imposed by the various terms used to define professional requirements in the context of the standards and regulations in which they appear.

Certain exceptions apply to these general rules, particularly in those circumstances in which the guide describes prevailing or preferred industry practices for the application of a standard or regulation. In these circumstances, the applicable senior committee responsible for reviewing the guide's content believes the guidance contained herein is appropriate for the circumstances.

Applicability of Quality Control Standards

QC section 10, *A Firm's System of Quality Control* (AICPA, *Professional Standards*), addresses a CPA firm's responsibilities for its system of quality control for its accounting and auditing practice. A system of quality control consists of policies that a firm establishes and maintains to provide it with reasonable assurance that the firm and its personnel comply with professional standards, as well as applicable legal and regulatory requirements. The policies also provide the firm with reasonable assurance that reports issued by the firm are appropriate in the circumstances.

QC section 10 applies to all CPA firms with respect to engagements in their accounting and auditing practice. In paragraph .06 of QC section 10, an *accounting and auditing practice* is defined as

> [a] practice that performs engagements covered by this section, which are audit, attestation, compilation, review, and any other services

for which standards have been promulgated by the AICPA Auditing Standards Board (ASB) or the AICPA Accounting and Review Services Committee (ARSC) under the "General Standards Rule" (ET sec. 1.300.001) or the "Compliance With Standards Rule" (ET sec. 1.310.001) of the AICPA Code of Professional Conduct. Although standards for other engagements may be promulgated by other AICPA technical committees, engagements performed in accordance with those standards are not encompassed in the definition of an *accounting and auditing practice.*"

In addition to the provisions of QC section 10, readers should be aware of other sections within AICPA *Professional Standards* that address quality control considerations, including the following provisions that address engagement level quality control matters for various types of engagements that an accounting and auditing practice might perform:

- AU-C section 220, *Quality Control for an Engagement Conducted in Accordance With Generally Accepted Auditing Standards* (AICPA, *Professional Standards*)
- AT-C section 105, *Concepts Common to All Attestation Engagements* (AICPA, *Professional Standards*)
- AR-C section 60, *General Principles for Engagements Performed in Accordance With Statements on Standards for Accounting and Review Services* (AICPA, *Professional Standards*)

Because of the importance of engagement quality, this guide includes appendix G, "Overview of Statements on Quality Control Standards." This appendix summarizes key aspects of the quality control standard. This summarization should be read in conjunction with QC section 10, AU-C section 220, AT-C section 105, AR-C section 60, and the quality control standards issued by the PCAOB, as applicable.

Independence

The practitioner performing an attestation engagement is required to be *independent* pursuant to the "Independence Rule" (AICPA, *Professional Standards*, ET sec. 1.200.001) of the AICPA Code of Professional Conduct, unless the practitioner is required by law or regulation to accept the engagement and report on the subject matter or assertion.[2]

AICPA.org Website

The AICPA encourages you to visit the website at www.aicpa.org, and the Financial Reporting Center at www.aicpa.org/FRC. The Financial Reporting Center supports members in the execution of high-quality financial reporting. Whether you are a financial statement preparer or a member in public practice, this center provides exclusive member-only resources for the entire financial reporting process, and provides timely and relevant news, guidance and examples supporting the financial reporting process. Another important focus of the Financial Reporting Center is keeping those in public practice up to date

---

[2] Paragraph .24 of AT-C section 105, *Concepts Common to All Attestation Engagements* (AICPA, *Professional Standards*).

on issues pertaining to preparation, compilation, review, audit, attestation, assurance, and advisory engagements. Certain content on the AICPA's websites referenced in this guide may be restricted to AICPA members only.

Select Recent Developments Significant to This Guide

Attestation Clarity Project

To address concerns over the clarity, length, and complexity of its standards, the ASB established clarity drafting conventions and undertook a project to redraft all the standards it issues in clarity format. The redrafting of SSAEs or attestation standards in SSAE No. 18 represents the culmination of that process.

The attestation standards are developed and issued in the form of SSAEs and are codified into sections. SSAE No. 18 recodifies the AT section numbers designated by SSAE Nos. 10–17 using the identifier AT-C.

TABLE OF CONTENTS

Chapter		Paragraph
1	Introduction to Sustainability Examination and Review Engagements	.01-.58
	Introduction to Using the Guide	.01-.04
	Introduction to Sustainability Information and Background	.05-.13
	Boundaries (Operational, Organizational, and Reporting Boundaries)	.08-.12
	Base Year Information	.13
	Measurement Uncertainty	.14-.21
	Objectives of an Examination of Sustainability Information	.22
	Objectives of a Review of Sustainability Information	.23
	Preconditions for an Examination or Review of Sustainability Information	.24-.50
	Assessing the Appropriateness of the Subject Matter	.27-.32
	Assessing the Suitability of the Applicable Criteria	.33-.38
	Assessing the Availability of Criteria	.39-.40
	Assessing the Ability to Obtain Evidence	.41-.44
	Other Preconditions	.45-.50
	Use of Other Practitioners	.51
	Agreeing on the Terms of the Engagement	.52-.56
	Requesting a Written Assertion	.57-.58
	Written Assertion by the Responsible Party	.58
2	Planning the Examination or Review Engagement	.01-.45
	Planning Considerations	.01-.02
	Nature and Characteristics of the Subject Matter	.03-.10
	Organization Structure and Nature of Business	.11-.13
	Organizational and Reporting Boundaries	.14-.15
	Characteristics of the Collection and Reporting Processes	.16-.19
	Consistency	.20
	Comparative Information	.21
	Internal Audit	.22
	Measurement Uncertainty	.23-.27
	Using the Work of an Other Practitioner	.25-.27
	Risk Assessment Procedures	.28-.32
	Materiality in Planning and Performing the Engagement	.33-.44
	Considerations When Selecting and Using the Work of a Practitioner's Specialist	.45
3	Performing Examination or Review Procedures	.01-.86
	Measurement Uncertainty	.07-.13
	Responding to Assessed Risks and Obtaining Evidence	.14-.17
	Procedures	.18-.30

Chapter		Paragraph
3	**Performing Examination or Review Procedures**—continued	
	Considerations Regarding Analytical Procedures	.24-.30
	Tests of Controls	.31-.33
	Procedures Other Than Tests of Controls	.34-.36
	Procedures Regarding Estimates and Measurement Uncertainty	.37-.40
	Sampling	.41-.43
	Fraud, Laws, and Regulations	.44-.45
	Revision of Risk Assessment	.46-.48
	Evaluating the Reliability of Information Produced by the Entity	.49-.52
	Using the Work of a Practitioner's Specialist or Internal Auditors	.53-.55
	Using the Work of an Other Practitioner	.56
	Evaluating the Results of Examination or Review Procedures	.57-.77
	Considering Subsequent Events and Subsequently Discovered Facts	.66-.67
	Consistency	.68-.77
	Written Representations	.78-.80
	Other Information	.81-.82
	Description of Criteria	.83-.85
	Disclosures of Management Interpretations of the Criteria	.85
	Documentation	.86
4	**Reporting on an Examination or Review Engagement**	.01-.49
	Forming an Opinion or Conclusion	.01-.09
	Measurement Uncertainty	.06-.09
	Preparing the Practitioner's Report	.10-.14
	Content of the Practitioner's Report	.15-.41
	Examination Reports	.15-.17
	Review Reports	.18-.20
	General Reporting Guidance	.21-.23
	Reporting Situations Applicable to Both Examination and Review Engagements	.24-.41
	Modified Opinions (Examinations)	.42-.43
	Modified Conclusions (Reviews)	.44-.45
	Correction of a Material Misstatement in Previously Issued Sustainability Information	.46-.49
5	**Performing an Examination or Review Engagement on Greenhouse Gas Emissions Information**	.01-.61
	Introduction to GHG Emissions Information	.03-.17
	GHG Emissions Reporting in the United States	.05

Table of Contents

Chapter		Paragraph
5	Performing an Examination or Review Engagement on Greenhouse Gas Emissions Information—continued	
	Terms and Definitions Used by Registries and Regulatory Frameworks	.06-.07
	Scopes for Reporting GHG Emissions: Direct and Indirect Emissions	.08
	Boundaries for GHG Emissions	.09-.11
	Base Year GHG Emissions	.12
	GHG Emission Reduction Projects	.13-.16
	Uncertainty in the Measurement of GHG Emissions	.17
	Objectives of an Examination of GHG Emissions Information	.18-.19
	GHG Emission Reduction Information	.19
	Objectives of a Review of GHG Emissions Information	.20-.21
	GHG Emission Reduction Information	.21
	Additional Considerations Regarding Preconditions for an Examination or Review of GHG Emissions Information	.22-.32
	Assessing the Appropriateness of the Subject Matter	.22-.24
	Assessing the Suitability of the Criteria—Additional Considerations Concerning GHG Emissions Information	.25-.26
	Assessing the Ability to Obtain Evidence—Additional Considerations Concerning GHG Emission Reduction Information	.27
	Other Preconditions	.28-.32
	Using the Work of an Other Practitioner for GHG Emissions Information	.33-.35
	Other Engagement Acceptance Considerations Regarding GHG Emissions Information	.36
	Requesting a Written Assertion on GHG Emissions Information	.37
	Planning the Examination or Review Engagement	.38-.39
	Obtaining an Understanding of GHG Emissions Information	.38
	Characteristics of the Collection and Reporting Processes—Consistency Considerations Regarding GHG Emissions Information	.39
	Potential Misstatements Relating to GHG Emissions Information	.40
	Considerations on Using the Work of a Practitioner's Specialist in a GHG Emissions Engagement	.41
	Illustrative Procedures	.42-.54
	Site Visits	.45-.46
	Corroboration	.47
	Techniques to Calculate GHG Emissions and Reductions	.48-.50
	Procedures Specific to GHG Emission Reduction Engagements	.51

©2017, AICPA

Chapter		Paragraph
5	**Performing an Examination or Review Engagement on Greenhouse Gas Emissions Information**—continued	
	Considering Subsequent Events	.52
	GHG Emissions Inventory	.53
	Evaluating or Considering Adequacy of Disclosure	.54
	Written Representations	.55
	Other Information	.56
	Documentation	.57
	Reporting Situations Applicable to Both Examination and Review Engagements	.58-.61
	References to the Report of an Other Practitioner in a GHG Emission Reduction Engagement	.58
	Significant Inherent Limitations	.59
	Matters of Emphasis	.60
	Comparative Information	.61

Appendix	
A	Illustrations of Measurements and Measurement Uncertainty
B	Characteristics of Sustainability Information and Illustrative Examination and Review Procedures
C	Illustrative Representation Letters and Additional Representations
D	Illustrative Practitioner's Examination Reports
E	Illustrative Practitioner's Review Reports
F	Illustrative Practitioner's Report on an Examination of One or More Specified Indicators and a Review of Others, Reporting on the Subject Matter, Unmodified Opinion and Unmodified Conclusion
G	Overview of Statements on Quality Control Standards

Glossary

Index of Pronouncements and Other Technical Guidance

Subject Index

Chapter 1

Introduction to Sustainability Examination and Review Engagements

Introduction to Using the Guide

1.01 *Sustainability information*,[1] as used in this guide, refers to information about sustainability matters (such as economic, environmental, social, and governance performance). Preparers of sustainability information often seek to increase the credibility of their reported sustainability information to users. Accordingly, they may engage practitioners to perform an attestation engagement or others to perform some form of assurance engagement. This guide is intended to assist practitioners in performing an attestation engagement in accordance with AICPA attestation standards on information that is held out as sustainability information, as discussed in paragraph 1.03.

1.02 Greenhouse gas (GHG) emissions information is one type of sustainability information for which practitioners are engaged to perform attestation engagements. As entities often prepare separate reports on GHG information, this guide includes specific guidance on application of AICPA attestation standards to such separate presentations in chapter 5. Such guidance is intended to supplement the general guidance throughout chapters 1–4 and, though specific to performing an attestation engagement on a separate presentation of GHG emissions information, can also be considered when performing an attestation engagement on a *sustainability report* that includes GHG emissions information.

1.03 This guide is applicable when the reporting entity is holding the subject matter out as sustainability information or makes an assertion that it is sustainability information. Examples of ways in which the reporting entity might hold out the subject matter as sustainability information include the following:

- Labeling the report containing the subject matter as a sustainability report, corporate social responsibility report, or environmental, social and governance report, or a similar title
- Labeling the presentation of information as a GHG emissions schedule or statement
- Submitting the presentation in response to a third-party requirement for the submission of sustainability information (for example, to sustainability rating bodies)
- Labeling sections of a broader report, such as in a report submitted to a securities regulator (for example, in the "Management Discussion and Analysis" section of an SEC Form 10-K), as sustainability, corporate social responsibility, or environmental, social and governance information

---

[1] Terms defined in the glossary are italicized the first time they appear in this guide.

- Labeling the subject matter appearing on the entity's website as sustainability, corporate social responsibility, or environmental, social and governance information, or a similar title
- Citing a sustainability framework, including standards, regulations, and entity-specific criteria for sustainability information, as criteria for the preparation or presentation of the subject matter

Given the varied nature of the subject matter, the practitioner may need to exercise judgment in ascertaining whether the guide is applicable to the engagement.

1.04 This chapter includes the following:

- Background on the subject matter of sustainability information
- Objectives of an examination or review of sustainability information under AICPA attestation standards
- Guidance on applying the engagement preconditions of AICPA attestation standards to a potential attestation engagement on sustainability information
- Guidance on agreeing to the terms of the engagement and requesting a written assertion with respect to sustainability information

Chapter 2 provides guidance on planning the attestation engagement on sustainability information. Chapter 3 provides guidance on performing the engagement, and chapter 4 provides guidance on forming an opinion or conclusion and reporting on an attestation engagement on sustainability information. Chapter 5 includes additional guidance specific to performing the engagement when the sustainability information is GHG emissions information as discussed in paragraph 1.02.

Introduction to Sustainability Information and Background

1.05 The following are examples of subject matter that might be addressed in an entity's sustainability information:

- Economic
    - Direct economic value generated and distributed, including to stakeholders other than shareholders
    - Financial implications and other risks or opportunities related to climate change, availability of resources, relationship with the workforce, and other environmental, social, and governance factors
    - Defined benefit plan obligations, and funding of such
    - Government-provided financial assistance
    - Market presence
    - Procurement practices, including with respect to supply chain compliance with the entity's policies and applicable laws and regulations

Introduction to Sustainability Examination and Review Engagements 3

- Environmental
  - Materials used, including future availability and dependability of sources of supply
  - Energy consumption, sources, and intensity
  - Water consumption, including future availability and dependability of sources of supply
  - Biodiversity, including impact of sources of supply on habitat
  - GHG emissions
  - Waste
  - Environmental compliance
  - Product stewardship
- Social
  - Occupational health and safety
  - Training and education of employees
  - Nondiscrimination, diversity, and equal opportunity employment
  - Equal remuneration based on the work performed, regardless of sex, race, national origin, religious belief, or sexual preference
  - Freedom of association and collective bargaining
  - Labor practices and grievance mechanisms
  - Child labor
  - Forced or compulsory labor
  - Labor management relations
  - Anticorruption
  - Customer health and safety
  - Product safety
  - Product and service labeling
  - Supply chain matters (for example, occupational health and safety, human rights, and labor practices of suppliers)
- Governance
  - Governance structure and composition
  - Role of highest governance body in various activities of the entity
  - Management and oversight of sustainability policies, practices, and risks

1.06 Sustainability information may be quantitative or qualitative in nature (for example, narrative or qualitative measures) and may be presented in various ways, including in a sustainability report, within an entity's annual

©2017, AICPA   AAG-SUST 1.06

report, as part of an integrated report, in a schedule or statement of GHG emissions information (referred to as a schedule of GHG emissions information throughout the remainder of this guide), or as a presentation of one or more *sustainability indicators* or *sustainability metrics*. At the date of publication of this guide, there is growing interest in sustainability reporting and other emerging types of external reporting (such as integrated reporting). Accordingly, the manner in which sustainability information is presented is evolving and new ways of reporting such information, including the creation of new standards and frameworks, are likely to emerge.

1.07 Various reporting frameworks or standards exist for sustainability information that provide criteria for what information is to be reported (for example, as to what information is to be included in a sustainability report or a schedule of GHG emission information); such frameworks or standards also may include criteria for how to measure the sustainability information. However, in the absence of measurement criteria in a specific reporting framework, entities may use such reporting framework or standard, together with other criteria. Paragraphs 1.33–.38 discuss assessing the suitability of the criteria. Given the varied nature of the subject matter and the criteria, a multidisciplinary team may be needed to perform the engagement. Paragraphs 1.24–.50 discuss preconditions for an examination or review engagement, including assessing the appropriateness of the subject matter and the suitability of the applicable criteria, professional competencies needed, and considering the use of a practitioner's specialist.

Boundaries (Operational, Organizational, and Reporting Boundaries)

1.08 Three different *boundaries* are often considered in sustainability reporting:

- *Organizational boundary.* The legal composition of an entity for which it has direct or operational control over the entity's activities; common approaches used for organizational boundaries include equity share, financial control and operational control.
- *Operational boundary.* Activities, including actions of third parties as a consequence of their interaction with the entity, that affect the entity's sustainability performance; an entity may recognize that its sustainability impacts and concerns extend beyond its organizational boundary—for example, GHG emissions of vendors (such as airlines or utility companies)—as a consequence of doing business with the entity.
- *Reporting boundary.* The boundary used by the entity to report its sustainability information; it may include direct and indirect effects including sustainability consequences of third parties that are within the entity's operational boundary.

1.09 The organizational boundary is used to identify the operations, facilities, and activities of the entity. In reporting on sustainability performance, an entity identifies its operational boundaries and activities within. These activities may occur within or beyond the organizational boundary.

1.10 Activities within the operational boundary include activities such as emission sources, water stream, waste, and employee categories associated with operations that are affected by such activities. The operational boundary can vary by sustainability indicator or subject matter. The entity chooses the scope of accounting and reporting for activities from within the operational boundary.

1.11 The reporting boundary for sustainability information can vary by sustainability indicator or subject matter. The reporting boundary may be the same as the organizational boundary (that is, includes the sustainability information for the entire entity); may be a subset within the organizational boundary (that is, includes sustainability information only for certain locations); or it may cover a portion of both the organizational and operational boundaries, as illustrated in figure 1.

Figure 1

Relationship Between Organizational, Operational, and Reporting Boundaries

Example 1—Reporting boundary includes all of the organization (the entity) and some of the operational impacts

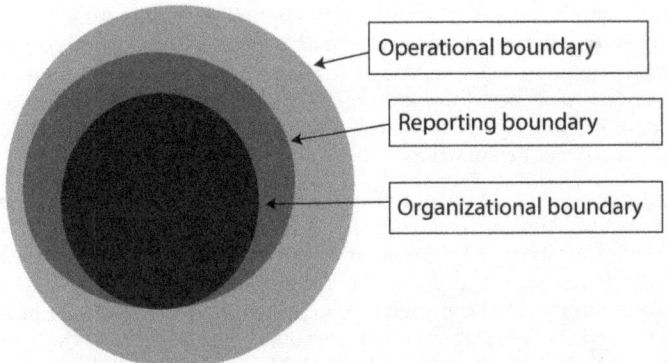

Example 2—The reporting boundary includes most, but not all, of the organization (the entity) and some of the operational impacts

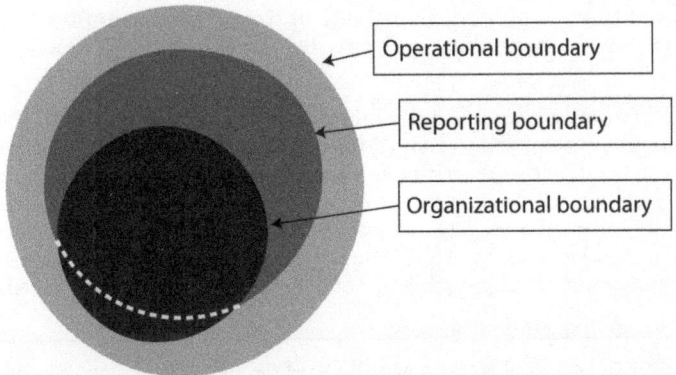

1.12 The boundaries used in reporting sustainability information may also be a function of the requirements of the intended users of the information and the criteria selected. For example, certain regulators may establish requirements for the boundaries to be used in reporting sustainability information to the respective regulator. Different criteria for measuring and reporting sustainability information may identify different boundaries to be used in reporting under the respective criteria.

Base Year Information

1.13 To show meaningful and consistent comparisons of sustainability metrics over time, entities often establish a *base year*. Sustainability information may be presented in relation to the base year, or comparative information for each year including and subsequent to the base year might be reported. For example, if the base year is 20x1, the entity might report comparative information in 20x5 for 20x1 through 20x4. Refer to paragraph 5.12 for discussion of base year GHG emissions.

Measurement Uncertainty

1.14 The outcome of the measurement of sustainability information is affected by the nature of the information, the method used to measure the sustainability information, how the method is applied, the competence and experience of the person making the *measurement*, and the *accuracy* and *precision*[2] of the tool or methodology used to make the measurement. *Measurement methods* include direct measurement (for example, a meter for water withdrawn or electricity used, or a truck scale for waste), measuring a surrogate activity (such as production data), and estimations.

1.15 Given the varied nature of sustainability information and the means in which such information is measured or estimated, many types of sustainability information cannot be measured with a high degree of accuracy. The inherent lack of accuracy and precision of the tool or methodology leads to *measurement uncertainty*. Measurement uncertainty is a characteristic of reported measured values that describes the dispersion of the quantities that could reasonably be attributed to the reported value. Measurement uncertainty in a reported value is reflective of incomplete knowledge inherent in the measurement process and, accordingly, includes estimation uncertainty. Uncertainty of measurement can result from random effects, in which repeated measurement gives a randomly different result for which the measurement uncertainty may be estimated through statistical methods; or from systematic effects, for which the measurement uncertainty may only be estimated through nonstatistical methods.

1.16 Generally, because of the inherent inaccuracy and imprecision of the measurement process, the range of measurement uncertainty cannot be reduced or removed by the practitioner via additional review or examination procedures. If the practitioner is aware of more accurate or precise measurement methods, the practitioner may suggest that management consider using such alternative measurement methods. But measurement of the reported information is management's responsibility, not the practitioner's. The practitioner is

---

[2] The terms *accuracy* and *precision* may be viewed synonymously in some contexts; however, these terms have different meanings for engineers and scientists. They look to the technical definition of *accuracy* as the closeness or degree to which a measurement conforms to the true or correct value, whereas *precision* is considered in terms of how repeatable the measurement can be made. Given the nature of the subject matter covered by this guide, the guide uses the technical definitions for these terms consistent with the definitions considered by engineers and scientists; please refer to the glossary.

Introduction to Sustainability Examination and Review Engagements

responsible for evaluating whether the disclosure of the methodology and related measurement uncertainty allows users to understand and compare the reported information from period to period and entity to entity.

1.17 Known errors are not considered part of measurement uncertainty. Similarly, the use of inappropriate measurement techniques, data, or assumptions—and the resulting errors—are also not considered part of measurement uncertainty.

1.18 The range of measurement uncertainty associated with a reported value may be insignificant or it may be quite high in relation to the reported information. A significant amount of measurement uncertainty often exists for certain sustainability information (for example, the measurement of GHG emissions or waste generation).

1.19 When it is determined that disclosure of a range would be useful in evaluating the reasonableness of a reported value, the range disclosed would encompass all reasonable outcomes rather than all possible outcomes. A range comprising all possible outcomes is too wide to be effectively used for evaluation purposes.

1.20 Measurement uncertainty around the actual value of the sustainability information may result from factors such as the following:

a. The accuracy and precision of the measurement tool and process

b. The potential use of incomplete data in measuring sustainability information, for example,
   i. measurements based on the extrapolation of sampled data;
   ii. compensation for missing data, such as making estimates to account for missing data from facilities that are unable to provide data or missing fuel bills;
   iii. the frequency of the measurement not being sufficient to account for all variability; and
   iv. measurements performed on other than the exact "cutoff" date and time for the subject matter reported

c. The accuracy and precision of conversion and other factors, for example,
   i. factors that are subject to a degree of uncertainty, such as factors used to calculate the number of units of methane (CH_4) and nitrous oxide (N_2O) resulting from the combustion of fossil fuels;
   ii. factors for the conversion of data to a standard format, such as factors used to convert units of CH_4 and N_2O to units of carbon dioxide (CO_2) based on their relative environmental impacts; or
   iii. average factors that are not perfectly matched to specific and varying circumstances, such as average miles per gallon and average number of kilograms of CO_2 emitted per megawatt hour of energy generated

d. The use of assumptions that simplify the calculation of highly complex processes

Appendix A illustrates measurements and measurement uncertainty for several examples of sustainability information.

1.21 When high measurement uncertainty exists, disclosure of its existence, together with a quantification of the uncertainty, such as the range of reasonable values for the measure, can provide meaningful information to intended users of the sustainability information regarding the *point value* reported. Chapters 2 and 3 discuss planning considerations and the nature of procedures performed concerning measurement uncertainty; chapter 4 discusses evaluating the adequacy of disclosures.

Objectives of an Examination of Sustainability Information

1.22 In conducting an examination of sustainability information, the objectives of the practitioner are to

   a. obtain reasonable assurance about whether the sustainability information as measured or evaluated against the criteria is free from material misstatement; and
   b. express an opinion in a written report about whether
      i. the sustainability information is presented in accordance with the criteria, in all material respects, or
      ii. the assertion is fairly stated, in all material respects.

Objectives of a Review of Sustainability Information

1.23 In conducting a review of sustainability information, the objectives of the practitioner are to

   a. obtain limited assurance about whether any material modifications should be made to the sustainability information in order for it to be presented in accordance with the criteria; and
   b. express a conclusion in a written report about whether the practitioner is aware of any material modifications that should be made to
      i. the sustainability information, in order for it to be presented in accordance with the criteria, or
      ii. the assertion, in order for it to be fairly stated.

Preconditions for an Examination or Review of Sustainability Information

1.24 In determining whether to accept an examination or review engagement, AT-C section 105, *Concepts Common to All Attestation Engagements*,[3]

---

[3] Paragraph .25*b*(i) of AT-C section 105, *Concepts Common to All Attestation Engagements*. All AT-C sections cited in this chapter can be found in AICPA *Professional Standards*.

Introduction to Sustainability Examination and Review Engagements

requires the practitioner to determine, among other preconditions, the following:

- That the subject matter is appropriate (paragraphs 1.27–.32 of this guide)
- That the criteria to be applied in the preparation and evaluation of the sustainability information are suitable and will be available to the intended users (paragraphs 1.33–.40)
- That the practitioner expects to be able to obtain the evidence needed to arrive at the practitioner's opinion or conclusion (paragraphs 1.41–.44)

AT-C section 105 contains guidance on each of the preconditions. This guide supplements such guidance with subject matter-specific considerations.

1.25 In determining whether it is appropriate to accept the attestation engagement, the practitioner also might consider whether other engagements previously performed covered the same subject matter. For example, if the practitioner has obtained reasonable assurance on a specified indicator in another engagement and reported on such specified indicator, the practitioner should be reporting at the same level of assurance on the specified indicator for the current engagement. If the practitioner is asked to review five *specified indicators* included in a sustainability report but has already audited or examined one of the five indicators in another engagement, the practitioner would be engaged to review the four indicators and to reissue the practitioner's examination report on the specified indicator on which the practitioner previously reported. However, if the practitioner previously performed a review of a specified indicator, the practitioner may subsequently be engaged to examine such indicator.

1.26 To the extent the sustainability information includes an element that was previously audited or examined as part of a broader engagement (for example, revenue previously audited as part of the financial statements taken as a whole, or *GHG emission reductions* previously examined as part of a GHG emissions statement), the element may either be examined or reviewed as part of the current engagement on the sustainability information. See paragraph 2.07 for further discussion in the context of planning the engagement.

Assessing the Appropriateness of the Subject Matter

1.27 The subject matter of an examination or review engagement relating to sustainability information may

- consist of specified indicators that are presented on their own or included as part of a sustainability report or other report;
- be a discrete section of a report covering an individual topic or category (for example, human rights, health and safety); or
- be the entire sustainability report.

If the subject matter is specified indicators, the practitioner may examine some of the specified indicators and review others. Also, the practitioner may review the entire sustainability report and examine some specified indicators within the reviewed sustainability report. The assessment of the appropriateness of the subject matter and the scope of the engagement, however, are independent of the determination of the level of service to be performed. Specifically, if the subject matter is not appropriate for an examination engagement, it is not appropriate for a review engagement.

1.28 Matters to consider in assessing whether the subject matter (for example, an entire sustainability report, a discrete section, or specified indicators) is appropriate for an examination or review engagement may include the following:

- The intended users' requirements and whether the sustainability information and the practitioner's report could be misleading (for example, an engagement to report on only the aspects of a sustainability program that have positive outcomes). A focus on intended users' needs can assist the practitioner in making professional judgments about the appropriateness of the subject matter.

- Whether any limitations on the reported information, as well as the reason therefor, will be clearly and transparently disclosed (for example, if the sustainability report does not address all relevant groups of users, does not include information for all countries in which the organization operates, or does not include all sustainability information and metrics of relevance and interest to users).

1.29 Users are typically interested not only in what is included in the sustainability information, but also whether material information has been omitted. For example, if an entity narrows the scope of an engagement to purposefully avoid reporting certain information, the subject matter may not be considered appropriate, particularly if the practitioner believes that the aspect to be examined or reviewed is not likely to meet the information needs of intended users. Accordingly, the practitioner might consider this in assessing whether the subject matter is appropriate for an examination or review engagement.

1.30 Performing an examination or review engagement on the entire sustainability report necessitates that the practitioner assess the completeness of the report, which could be highly subjective. Limiting the examination or review engagement to specified indicators appearing within a sustainability report may necessitate that the practitioner (1) assess the risk that the practitioner's conclusion or opinion could be construed to apply to more than the specified indicators, and (2) consider whether the entity may have selected the specified indicators to achieve favorable results in the attestation engagement rather than selecting the entire sustainability report for the engagement subject matter.

1.31 As described in paragraph .A41 of AT-C section 105, in determining whether the requested subject matter exhibits the characteristic of appropriate subject matter for attestation engagement purposes, it may be appropriate when the examination or review engagement relates to only one part of a broader subject matter for the practitioner to consider whether information about the aspect that the practitioner is asked to examine or review is likely to meet the information needs of intended users.

1.32 Determination of the appropriateness of the subject matter also may need to be considered in conjunction with evaluating the suitability of the criteria.

Assessing the Suitability of the Applicable Criteria

1.33 AT-C section 105 states that suitable criteria exhibit all of the following characteristics:

Introduction to Sustainability Examination and Review Engagements

- **Relevance.** Criteria are relevant to the subject matter.
- **Objectivity.** Criteria are free from bias.
- **Measurability.** Criteria permit reasonably consistent measurements, qualitative or quantitative, of subject matter.
- **Completeness.** Criteria are complete when subject matter prepared in accordance with them does not omit relevant factors that could reasonably be expected to affect decisions of the intended users made on the basis of that subject matter.[4]

1.34 A factor that may affect measurability of the sustainability information is the degree of specificity of the applicable sustainability reporting framework (for example, the criteria for determining what topics should be addressed in the sustainability information and how the sustainability results should be measured).

1.35 In addition, there may be instances in which disclosures that are not required by the criteria nevertheless may be necessary for the sustainability information to be useful, understandable and comparable to intended users, such as disclosures about the following:

- The methodology applied in measuring the subject matter
- Measurement methods such as using a meter or indirectly measuring the subject matter via a surrogate activity that is correlated with the subject matter being measured (for example, measuring miles flown, which is correlated with emissions of certain greenhouse gases)
- Significant assumptions and other factors used in making the measurement or evaluation
- Sources of inherent limitations on accuracy and the extent of high measurement uncertainty

In assessing the suitability of the criteria, the practitioner considers what disclosure requirements exist in the criteria and whether the entity-specific situation might necessitate additional disclosure beyond what is specified in the criteria. The need or potential need for disclosures not specified in the criteria does not necessarily make the criteria unsuitable or preclude a practitioner from examining or reviewing such information. Nor does the existence of high measurement uncertainty necessarily make the criteria unsuitable or the subject matter inappropriate.

1.36 Criteria for measuring or evaluating qualitative information (for example, statements about employee safety or satisfaction) may not be sufficiently measurable to permit reasonably consistent measurements or evaluations of the subject matter, for example, because the criteria may be subject to varying interpretations. Statements such as 'we are an ethical company,' 'we provide a safe working environment for all our employees,' or 'our employee survey indicates that our people are highly engaged and motivated' are not capable of measurement or evaluation in an examination or review engagement unless the entity can clearly articulate the criteria used to measure or evaluate the subject matter as evidence for these statements, and such criteria allow for a consistent evaluation of the subject matter.

---

[4] Paragraph .A42 of AT-C section 105.

1.37 An entity might use more than one set of criteria for the measurement and presentation of the sustainability information. For example, an entity might use the guidelines published by the Global Reporting Initiative for purposes of presenting its sustainability report and also use other criteria for measuring certain information reported therein (for example, the World Resources Institute/World Business Council for Sustainable Development Greenhouse Gas Protocol for GHG measurements).[5] As discussed in paragraph 1.35, specific disclosures regarding how the sustainability information has been measured against the criteria (such as the methodologies applied, the measurement methods, assumptions, estimates, and factors used in making the measurement or evaluation and the extent of high measurement uncertainty) may be necessary in the presentation. When the criteria permit the selection from alternatives, the practitioner might consider whether there is bias in the entity's selection and consistency of the criteria from the prior year. Considerations as to how such criteria and any specific disclosures are then made available to the intended users is discussed in paragraphs 1.39–.40.

1.38 If the examination or review engagement relates to the entire sustainability report, a consideration in assessing the suitability of the applicable criteria might include whether the criteria to assess every material element of the sustainability report can be identified and disclosed. (Note: What constitutes a material element of the sustainability report might need to be carefully considered in the context of qualitative information, particularly where numerical benchmarks do not apply.)

Assessing the Availability of Criteria

1.39 AT-C section 105 cites various means by which criteria may be made available. When criteria used are not publicly available (for example, when management has developed its own criteria or supplemented publicly available criteria with specific disclosures regarding how the sustainability information has been measured against the criteria as discussed in paragraph 1.37), the criteria often are included in, or accompany (for example, in an exhibit), the sustainability information. Alternatively, the criteria might be included in or be attached to the practitioner's report. Such criteria could also be made available by posting the criteria to the entity's website; however, care by the entity would need to be exercised that such criteria remain available as long as the sustainability information to which it pertains and the practitioner's report thereon is made available. The practitioner may include a provision in the engagement letter regarding management's responsibility to make the criteria available (see paragraph 1.52).

1.40 In assessing the availability of management-developed criteria, the practitioner may consider matters such as the following:

- Whether the description of the criteria to be made available will provide sufficient information for intended users to understand how the sustainability information was measured (for example, the indicators included in the sustainability information) or in the

---

[5] A variety of different sustainability reporting standards and frameworks exist and are continually evolving (such as sustainability standards of the Global Reporting Initiative [GRI] and the Sustainability Accounting Standards Board [SASB]). Any frameworks or standards referenced in this guide are provided for illustrative purposes only and are not intended to reflect endorsements of the particular standards or frameworks. Furthermore, the examples provided are not intended to reflect a complete list of all sustainability accounting standards and frameworks.

Introduction to Sustainability Examination and Review Engagements

case of a sustainability report or section of the report, how material matters were identified for inclusion in the sustainability report
- Whether the manner of presenting the criteria will facilitate identification of such criteria in the practitioner's report
- If the criteria are to be posted to the entity's website, the risk that the criteria would not remain available as discussed in paragraph 1.39

Assessing the Ability to Obtain Evidence

1.41 In a sustainability examination or review engagement, the party requesting such engagement may not be responsible for the sustainability information and, accordingly, may not have the ability to provide access to the related records or to provide the representations that the practitioner may consider necessary (for example, someone in investor relations might request the engagement, but not be responsible for the information to be reported and thus may not be in the position to provide certain representations; there also may be challenges in the practitioner obtaining access to evidence from those who are responsible). As a result, the nature of the relationship between the party requesting the engagement and the responsible party may be a relevant consideration when determining whether or not to accept the engagement.

1.42 Examples of other factors that are relevant in determining whether the evidence needed to arrive at the practitioner's opinion or conclusion is likely to be available include the following:
- Whether the entity is likely to have adequate information systems, processes, and controls that provide an adequate data trail from initial measurement to final reporting to produce reliable information
- The accessibility of information from relevant third parties (for example, entities that are within the operational boundary, but not within the organizational boundary)
- Whether the information is expected to have been retained, particularly if there has been a significant passage of time between the period covered or "as of" date of the subject matter and the performance of the examination or review engagement (for example, for base year information)

1.43 If the examination or review engagement relates to the entire sustainability report, matters to consider might include the following:
- Whether adequate evidence in support of every material qualitative and quantitative statement included in the sustainability report can be obtained
- Whether adequate evidence can be obtained regarding the completeness of the sustainability report (that is, whether it provides a balanced and reasonable representation of the entity's sustainability performance, and does not omit any material element, either in terms of its boundaries or the sustainability information)

1.44 The following are examples of situations that may increase the risk that adequate evidence may not be available to accept an attestation engagement regarding sustainability information:

- The entity has changed measurement methods from one period to the next (see paragraph 5.39 for guidance relating to GHG emissions).
- The practitioner is engaged to perform the attest service at a date considerably later than the base year, which is also to be covered by the engagement (see paragraph 5.12 for a discussion of base years for GHG emissions).

Other Preconditions

Independence

1.45 The practitioner performing an attestation engagement is required to be independent pursuant to the "Independence Rule" (AICPA, *Professional Standards*, ET sec. 1.200.001) of the AICPA Code of Professional Conduct, unless the practitioner is required by law or regulation to accept the engagement and report on the subject matter or assertion.[6]

Professional Competence

1.46 AT-C section 105 also states that the practitioner should accept an examination or review engagement only when the engagement partner[7] is satisfied that those persons who are to perform the engagement (including any practitioner's external specialists) collectively have the appropriate competence and capabilities, including knowledge of the subject matter and capabilities to (1) perform the engagement in accordance with professional standards and applicable legal and regulatory requirements and (2) enable the issuance of a practitioner's report that is appropriate in the circumstances.[8]

1.47 When considering the competence and capabilities of engagement team members, the engagement partner might consider, among other matters, whether the team assigned to the engagement collectively has, or can acquire through appropriate training or participation, the following:

- An understanding of, and experience with, attestation engagements of a similar nature and complexity
- Knowledge of the entity's industry and business, including whether the industry in which the entity operates is subject to specific types of or unusual risks relating to the sustainability information
- Knowledge of relevant measurement methodologies, systems, processes, and technology used to measure, accumulate, and report the sustainability information
- An understanding of professional standards, and the ability to apply professional judgment in the sustainability attestation examination
- An understanding of legal and regulatory requirements relating to reporting sustainability information relevant to the engagement

---

[6] Paragraph .24 of AT-C section 105.
[7] See definition of *engagement partner* in paragraph .10 of AT-C section 105.
[8] Paragraphs .27*b* and .32*a* of AT-C section 105.

Introduction to Sustainability Examination and Review Engagements 15

In addition, the engagement partner should be satisfied that those involved in the engagement have been informed of their responsibilities, including the objectives of the procedures that they are to perform and matters that may affect the nature, timing, and extent of such procedures.[9]

Considering Use of a Practitioner's Specialist

1.48 As indicated in paragraph 1.05, sustainability information can comprise many types of information, not all of which may be in the field of the engagement partner's expertise. Accordingly, examination and review engagements on sustainability information may include significant use of specialists (for example, engineers or scientists). As a result, evidence might be obtained through the use of one or more practitioner's specialists (which may be a practitioner's internal specialist or a practitioner's external specialist.[10] Factors that might be considered by the engagement partner in determining whether to accept the engagement include the extent to which one or more practitioner's specialists might be needed in the performance of the examination or review engagement and whether the practitioner has or can obtain a sufficient understanding of the subject matter to be able to understand and evaluate the specialist's work as it relates to obtaining evidence for the examination or review engagement.

1.49 If a practitioner's internal specialist is to be used, the engagement partner should consider

- the professional competence and capabilities of such internal specialist as discussed in paragraphs 1.46–.47 in assigning responsibilities to the internal specialist and
- the firm's system of quality control for assigning review responsibilities in relation to such internal specialist's work.

1.50 If a practitioner's external specialist is to be used, the engagement partner should consider whether the engagement team will be able to be involved in the work of the external specialist to an extent that is sufficient for the engagement partner to accept responsibility for the engagement. Such determination is a matter of professional judgment, considering factors such as the materiality of the information for which the practitioner's external specialists are used (including the nature and magnitude of the specialists' work in relation to the overall engagement), the extent of such external specialists' work, and the extent of other evidence obtained.

Use of Other Practitioners

1.51 AT-C section 105 includes requirements for when the practitioner expects to use the work of an other practitioner,[11] including when the practitioner expects to assume responsibility for the work of the other practitioner.[12] For example, an other practitioner might be used in sustainability reporting when such other practitioner is engaged to examine or review sustainability information of a subsidiary and is to issue a report on such subsidiary's information. In such case, consistent with AT-C section 105, the engagement partner should

---

[9] Paragraph .32c of AT-C section 105.
[10] See definition of *practitioner's specialist* in paragraph .10 of AT-C section 105.
[11] See definition of an *other practitioner* in paragraph .10 of AT-C section 105.
[12] See paragraph .31 of AT-C section 105 for the requirements.

©2017, AICPA

consider whether the engagement team will be able to be involved in the work of the other practitioner to an extent that is sufficient to accept responsibility for the work of the other practitioner or whether reference might be made to the other practitioner in the practitioner's report.

Agreeing on the Terms of the Engagement

1.52 AT-C sections 205, *Examination Engagements*, and 210, *Review Engagements*, require that the practitioner agree upon the terms of the engagement with the engaging party and specify the terms that should be included in the engagement letter or other suitable form of written agreement.[13] When performing an examination or review of sustainability information, the agreed-upon terms of the engagement also may include the following:

    a. When the practitioner will be reporting on specified indicators, that management is responsible for determining which specified indicators are to be included in the scope of the engagement.

    b. That management agrees to include the practitioner's report with the related sustainability information if management indicates in such information that it has been the subject of an examination or review engagement performed by the practitioner's firm.

    c. If the criteria are not otherwise publicly available, that management acknowledges that the entity will make the criteria continuously available so long as the sustainability information is made available.

    d. That the responsible party agrees to provide a written assertion (see paragraphs 1.57–.58).

1.53 When an examination of some specified indicators is to be performed and a review of others, the engagement letter should clearly articulate which indicators are the subject matter of the examination engagement and which are the subject matter of the review engagement.

1.54 Considerations in agreeing on the terms of the engagement include the following:

- Whether the individual to sign the engagement letter or other form of agreement can serve as the responsible party (for example, whether the individual has the responsibility and authority within the entity to agree to the terms and make the necessary representations and assertions—see paragraph 1.41)

- Whether and in what manner the practitioner's report is to be included with the sustainability information

- The form of the subject matter (for example, whether an online, web-based report or a PDF posted to the entity's website) and the potential risks that the practitioner's report could be believed to cover more than intended (for example, if a web-based form of a sustainability report that includes symbols to indicate the specific information that was the subject of the engagement is to be used, there is the risk that the practitioner's report may not be

---

[13] Paragraphs .07–.09 of AT-C section 205, *Examination Engagements*, and paragraphs .08–.10 of AT-C section 210, *Review Engagements*, respectively.

Introduction to Sustainability Examination and Review Engagements

posted for the duration of the posting of the sustainability report and therefore may not be available to the users)

1.55 Online, web-based sustainability information also runs the risk of being updated without the practitioner's knowledge. Accordingly, as part of agreeing on the terms of the engagement, the practitioner might establish an understanding with the client regarding the conditions that are to exist for the practitioner's report to be posted to the entity's website and the protocol for notification of the practitioner by the client in the event of any changes.

1.56 As the manner in which sustainability information is presented varies, as discussed in paragraph 1.54, obtaining an acknowledgement before the commencement of the engagement about whether management agrees to include the practitioner's report with the related sustainability information if management indicates in such information that it has been subjected to an examination or review engagement and to make the criteria available helps avoid misunderstandings.

Requesting a Written Assertion

1.57 Whether reporting directly on the subject matter or a written assertion, as required under AT-C sections 205 and 210, the practitioner should request from the responsible party a written assertion about the measurement or evaluation of the subject matter against the applicable criteria.[14] The responsible party for sustainability information ordinarily is management of the entity reporting such information.

Written Assertion by the Responsible Party

1.58 A written assertion provided by the responsible party may be presented to a practitioner in a number of ways, such as in a narrative description, within a schedule, or as part of a representation letter appropriately identifying what is being presented and the point in time or period of time covered. Examples of written assertions on sustainability information are as follows:

- XYZ Company asserts that its sustainability report for the year ended December 31, 20XX, is [presented][15] in accordance with [*identify criteria selected by the responsible party*].
- XYZ Company's labor statistics included in [*identify title of report*] are calculated in accordance with [*identify criteria selected by the responsible party*].

Refer to paragraph 3.78 for guidance concerning obtaining assertions in the representation letter.

---

[14] Paragraph .10 of AT-C section 205 and paragraph .11 of AT-C section 210, respectively.

[15] Typically, sustainability information is in the form of a presentation and, accordingly, management might make an assertion that it is "presented in accordance with" the identified criteria.

Chapter 2

Planning the Examination or Review Engagement

Planning Considerations

2.01 In planning and performing an examination or review engagement, AT-C sections 205, *Examination Engagements*, and 210, *Review Engagements*, state, among other things, that the practitioner should do the following:

    a. In an examination, identify the characteristics of the engagement that define its scope and ascertain the reporting objectives of the engagement in order to plan the timing of the engagement and the nature of the communications required, and consider the factors that, in the practitioner's judgment, are significant in directing the engagement team's efforts.[1]

    b. In a review, obtain an understanding of the subject matter and other engagement circumstances sufficient to provide a basis for designing and performing procedures in order to achieve the objectives of the engagement. That understanding should include the practices used to measure, recognize and record the subject matter.[2]

2.02 Understanding the subject matter and other engagement circumstances in a sustainability examination or review engagement includes developing an understanding of the following:

    a. The nature and characteristics of the subject matter, discussed in paragraphs 2.03–.10 of this guide

    b. The organization's structure and nature of the entity's business, discussed in paragraphs 2.11–.13

    c. The entity's organizational and operational boundaries and its approach to setting reporting boundaries, including the reporting boundary used by the entity to prepare the sustainability information, discussed in paragraphs 2.14–.15

    d. The criteria used, the responsible party's interpretation of the criteria, and the availability of the criteria to measure particular components of and to present the sustainability information. (See paragraphs 1.33–.40 for considerations in assessing the suitability and availability of the criteria as part of the preconditions for accepting an examination or review engagement of sustainability information. During planning, the practitioner would consider whether the practitioner's initial assessment regarding the suitability and availability of the criteria has been reaffirmed or contradicted.)

    e. Definitions of key terms used and assumptions made with respect to material components of the sustainability information

---

[1] Paragraphs .11–.13 of AT-C section 205, *Examination Engagements*. All AT-C sections cited in this chapter can be found in AICPA *Professional Standards*.

[2] Paragraphs .12–.13 of AT-C section 210, *Review Engagements*.

f. The characteristics of the collection and reporting process of material components of the sustainability information, discussed in paragraphs 2.16–.19

g. Whether the criteria, measurement method (including methodology and conversion factors used), reporting boundary, or measurement units employed are consistent with that of the prior period, discussed in paragraph 2.20

h. Whether comparative information is presented and, if so, whether it is to be covered by the current examination or review engagement, or whether it was previously subjected to an examination or review engagement, discussed in paragraph 2.21

i. Whether the entity's internal audit function (or similar function) is relevant to the engagement, discussed in paragraph 2.22

j. Whether high measurement uncertainty exists in any of the quantitative sustainability information, discussed in paragraphs 2.23–.24

k. Whether the practitioner expects to use the work of an other practitioner, discussed in paragraphs 2.25–.27

l. Whether the practitioner expects to use the work of a practitioner's specialist, discussed in paragraph 2.45

Nature and Characteristics of the Subject Matter

2.03 The nature of planning will vary according to the nature and characteristics of the subject matter and the scope of the engagement. The following are examples:

- Sustainability information related to biodiversity is likely to require more extensive procedures on measurement uncertainty and the methodologies for capturing and reporting such information than sustainability information related to health and safety or employment practices.

- Materiality considerations will vary depending on whether the engagement is to include the entire sustainability report, a presentation of GHG emissions information, an identifiable section of a sustainability report, or only specified indicators. (Refer to the "Materiality in Planning and Performing the Engagement" section of this guide [paragraphs 2.33–.44] for more information.)

2.04 Some engagements address only an identifiable section(s) or specified indicators, but the practitioner's report is to appear in a document, such as a sustainability report, that also contains information that is not subject to the engagement. In such circumstances, the practitioner may develop an understanding of the information to be included in the entire document by reading a preliminary draft of the document or the prior year document to identify any potential matters, such as other related disclosures, to be taken into consideration in planning the examination or review engagement.

2.05 The characteristics of the sustainability information affect the availability of sufficient evidence and the nature of the procedures to be performed. Sustainability information may have one or more of the following characteristics:

Planning the Examination or Review Engagement

- Quantified information—Numerical information including statistics, which may be produced internally (such as derived from the entity's reporting system) or obtained externally (such as from other organizations outside its organizational boundary but within its operational boundary). These quantified indicators may be subject to high degrees of accuracy and precision[3] (low measurement uncertainty) or the tool or methodology used to arrive at such quantifications may be subject to lower degrees of accuracy or precision (and may result in high measurement uncertainty). Some quantified indicators, such as those related to future-oriented matters (for example, amounts specified as targets or goals) cannot be measured but may be supported by other types of evidence, such as board meeting minutes and policy statements.
- Factual narrative—Nonnumerical information that is supported by events that have occurred and is objectively determinable; it may be evidenced in various ways, including through reporting systems and the entity's internally produced reports from such systems or in information externally reported by other organizations. This includes directional indications of an effect or anticipated outcome (for example, increase or decrease, favorable or unfavorable).
- Soft narrative—Nonnumerical information that is subjective; it may contain views or judgments of management and those charged with governance but the substance of the narrative may be supported in the entity's operating practices and by various reports, internal communications, and the entity's internal or external websites.
- Diagrams or graphs—May be used as pictorial representations in conjunction with or instead of a narrative, schedule or table. These can be representations of quantified measurements and factual information or may be representative of soft narrative information.

2.06 If the engagement is for specified indicators, only certain of these characteristics may be present. However, if the subject matter of the examination or review engagement is an entire sustainability report or an identifiable section(s), all of these characteristics might be present. The practitioner should consider whether the characteristics present are consistent with the criteria.

2.07 When the engagement is to include financial-related matters, and the practitioner is also the financial statement auditor, the knowledge obtained from the financial statement audit and, if applicable, other services provided to the entity may be beneficial in planning the examination or review engagement. If the practitioner has not audited the financial statements, the practitioner may give consideration as to how the work of the financial statement auditor or other attest service providers may be used for purposes of obtaining appropriate evidence for financial-related and other matters included in the sustainability report that is the subject of the examination or review engagement. However, in considering the use of evidence obtained in conjunction with a financial statement audit, the practitioner should consider materiality for the subject matter

---

[3] Refer to the footnote to paragraph 1.14 regarding the use in this guide of the technical definitions for *accuracy* and *precision* that are common for engineers and scientists.

of the attestation engagement (see paragraphs 2.33–.44). Matters to consider may include whether the reporting boundaries are the same and whether the materiality applied in the audit of the financial statements affects the sufficiency of evidence obtained for purposes of the attestation engagement. Because the materiality thresholds may be different, the practitioner may need to supplement the audit or attest procedures with additional procedures to obtain sufficient evidence for the examination or review engagement.

2.08 If the subject matter is narrative information, the practitioner's procedures would involve obtaining assurance concerning management's basis for such statements. Narrative information can run the risk of being misleading (intentionally or unintentionally) through the words chosen, the tone of the statement, or the omission of material information concerning the matter. For example, the entity's description of its approach to managing risks might be inadequate.

2.09 If the subject matter includes forward-looking information, whether narrative or quantified information, the practitioner's procedures would involve obtaining assurance concerning the reasonableness of the assumptions used and the adequacy of disclosures around the assumptions in light of the criteria used by management; the practitioner is not responsible for the achievement of the future outlook.

2.10 Appendix B, "Characteristics of Sustainability Information and Illustrative Examination and Review Procedures," illustrates the manner in which the characteristics of sustainability information described in paragraph 2.05 apply to sustainability information, together with illustrative examination procedures for an examination engagement and review procedures for a review engagement of an entire sustainability report.

Organization Structure and Nature of Business

2.11 Obtaining an understanding of the entity's structure and nature of the business is important to being able to examine or review sustainability information. Accordingly, it is important to understand characteristics about the entity, including the following:

- The legal entities comprising the entity, its organizational boundary, and its governance
- Whether it has operations in multiple locations, and the types of products and services it offers
- The underlying business processes
- Significant changes thereto since the prior period

2.12 Sources of information to obtain the understanding include the following:

- Inquiries of management
- The entity's website and, in particular, the sustainability site, which can provide information about the entity's structure, vision, products, and services, as well as key stakeholders and how sustainability relates to its strategy
- Internal documents of the entity that discuss strategy

Planning the Examination or Review Engagement

- Minutes of the board and committee meetings
- Other entity documents

2.13 The extent to which the practitioner reads the information described in paragraph 2.12 may vary according to the following:

- The organizational, operational, and reporting boundaries (see paragraphs 2.14–.15)
- Whether the subject matter of the engagement is an entire sustainability report, a presentation of GHG emissions information, an identifiable section of a sustainability report or specified indicators
- Whether an examination or a review is being conducted

Organizational and Reporting Boundaries

2.14 Paragraphs 1.08–.12 provide an overview on boundaries. Understanding the organizational and reporting boundaries of the entity and considering whether the entity selects a consistent approach for consolidating data and other sustainability information similar to its treatment in the entity's financial statements may assist in identifying risks and planning appropriate procedures. For example, if the entity reports sustainability information only for a particular region, understanding the reporting boundary may include consideration of the reason the entity has chosen to narrow its reporting boundary (for example, narrowing the boundary in an effort to exclude poorly performing regions may not be appropriate). In contrast, if the entity broadens its reporting boundary for sustainability information to include information from within its operational boundary (for example, to include information on the life cycle of its products and from its key suppliers), relevant considerations may include what and how such information is obtained by the entity.

2.15 Understanding boundaries includes determining, usually through inquiry of management, whether there have been any changes in the organizational, operational, or reporting boundaries from the prior period and, if so, the reasons for such changes. Paragraphs 3.05E and 3.17E discuss the practitioner's consideration of reporting boundary in assessing risks of material misstatement in an examination; paragraphs 3.04R and 3.17R are applicable for procedures concerning the reporting boundary in a review engagement.

Characteristics of the Collection and Reporting Processes

2.16 Consistent with the requirements in AT-C sections 205 and 210 to obtain an understanding of the subject matter,[4] an understanding of the collection and reporting processes of material components of the sustainability information should be obtained, including which functions of the entity are responsible for these processes and the methodology used by management to determine what was considered material versus immaterial for reporting purposes. The determination of what constitutes a material component of sustainability information will vary according to the subject matter and by industry.

2.17 The characteristics of the information systems, processes, and controls over the sustainability information may affect the accuracy, completeness,

---

[4] Paragraph .15 of AT-C section 205 and paragraph .13 of AT-C section 210.

and reliability of the information produced and thus are relevant when planning and performing the engagement. Examples of characteristics that might be considered include the following:

- The complexity and number of the information systems and processes applicable to the collection, aggregation, and reporting of the sustainability information, and the frequency with which the systems and processes operate
- The existence, suitability of design, and effectiveness of controls over the collection, aggregation and reporting processes of the sustainability information and the frequency in which the controls operate
- Where the records for the sustainability information reside

2.18 If collecting and reporting sustainability information is a relatively new activity for the entity, the information systems, processes, and controls over the sustainability information may not be fully developed and may consist of both automated and manual processes. Some information may be initially gathered electronically and then used in a manual process, particularly if information is obtained from different systems. Relevant considerations may include whether any of the following situations are present and the effects that any such situation(s) might have on planning and performing the examination or review engagement:

- Systems and processes have been designed for purposes other than reporting information about sustainability; in such cases, they may not capture all the required information.
- Systems and processes that produce the sustainability information are not traditional accounting systems and processes and, therefore, have not been previously subject to assessment (for example, by internal audit or in conjunction with external audit or attest services); in such cases, they may not produce or contain the necessary documentation.
- Systems and processes capturing measurements are complex and involve highly technical information involving engineering and other science skills; in such cases, specialized skills may be necessary.
- Systems for capturing sustainability information are not subject to the same backup requirements or information technology general controls as traditional accounting systems and, therefore, data and subsequent system reports may not be complete or accurate.

2.19 A common concern with respect to the reliability of sustainability information is completeness, and with respect to any specific sustainability metric, the focus is ordinarily on the completeness of the inputs used to determine the sustainability metric. Additionally, in considering the entity's systems, processes, and controls, there may be heightened risk of human error in calculations or deficiencies in *internal control*. Examples of aspects of the collection and reporting processes that could lead to risks of material misstatement with respect to certain sustainability metrics include the following:

Planning the Examination or Review Engagement

- Economic
  - Identification of risks and opportunities posed by climate change may be incomplete.
  - Identification of sources of financial assistance received from governments may be incomplete.
  - Percentage of salary contributed to pension plans by employees or the entity may be incorrectly calculated due to errors in accumulating salary amounts.
- Governance
  - Statistics of the composition of the highest governing board are incorrectly calculated as a result of errors in gathering and accumulating information manually and the lack of adequate review of manual processes.
  - Identification of critical concerns communicated to the highest governance body may be incomplete.
- Water usage and discharge
  - Identification of the water sources may be incomplete. For example, water use may not be limited to metered supply from a supply company; it may include surface or groundwater, or the removal of water from a river for use in the entity's process (for example, cooling).
  - The water meters may not be accurate, as the accuracy depends on regular calibration and maintenance.
  - Identification of or accounting for pipe or body of water leakage rates may be incomplete or inaccurate, and estimates may be required.
  - The entity's evaluation may not address evaporation or employ accurate evaporation rates.
  - There may be regulatory considerations over discharged water and potential water pollution, such as location of facility, wastewater temperature, waste contaminants, or endangered or protected species.
  - The water usage reported may not be accurately converted from the units it is collected in (collection units) into the units it is to be reported in (reported units).
- Waste measurement
  - Identification of waste, reuse, and recycling sources may be incomplete and definitions may vary or be inconsistent, depending on national definitions and protocols.
  - If waste is weighed as the means by which data is collected, the waste scale may be inaccurate. There also may be risks related with who is responsible for the measurement, such as for landfill waste: If the entity is responsible for measurement, there may be a risk of understatement; and if the waste contractor is responsible for the measurement, there may be a risk of overstatement.

- The measurement methodology may not be consistent between locations.
- The length of time the waste has been stored could distort the data.
- There may be regulatory considerations (for example, related to hazardous materials).
- Sources for estimation factors may be unreliable (for example, lack of documented source) or vary from industry averages.

- Health and safety
  - Identification of actual incidents reported may be incomplete as it is often dependent on timely voluntary reporting by employees and contractors.
  - There may be performance incentives for lower incident rates.
  - There may be industry or territorial differences that are "acceptable" for not reporting such incidents.
  - There may be information obtained from a service organization.
  - There may be regulatory considerations (for example, compliance with child labor and minimum wage laws under the Occupational Safety and Health Administration [OSHA]) that could result in the status of incidents changing over time, such as OSHA recordables versus non-recordables, depending on the scope of the sustainability information being reported).

- GHG emissions
  - Identification of GHG-emitting sources may be incomplete.
  - Identification of all types of GHG emissions may be incomplete (for example, omission of methane emissions).
  - If measurements or calculations are performed manually, there is risk of human error.
  - Incorrect or outdated GHG emission factors may be used.
  - Identification of or accounting for *leakage* may be incomplete or inaccurate.
  - The base year may need to be adjusted for events such as sales or acquisitions of GHG-emitting sources.
  - There may be double counting of a GHG emission source within the entity.
  - There may be regulatory considerations providing incentive to falsify GHG emissions.
  - Renewable energy sources may not be considered, resulting in an overstatement of GHG emissions.

Consistency

2.20 If the criteria, the responsible party's interpretation of the criteria, or other matters have changed during the current year, matters that should be considered by the practitioner include the appropriateness of the change, the adequacy of disclosure regarding the change, implications on whether procedures are to be applied to amounts for prior periods that will be covered by the practitioner's updated opinion or conclusion, if applicable, and the implications on the practitioner's report, if any. Paragraphs 3.68–.73 discuss evaluating consistency for examination and review engagements.

Comparative Information

2.21 If sustainability information for a prior period was initially subject to the practitioner's prior engagement but additional disclosures for such information are included in the current period for such prior period(s), the practitioner may need to perform additional procedures in order to cover such new prior period disclosures in the practitioner's report. However, if the practitioner is not engaged to report on comparative information in the current period and the prior information has changed, the practitioner should inquire as to the reasons for the change to determine the effect on the reporting for the current period.

Internal Audit

2.22 Activities similar to those performed by an internal audit function may be conducted by functions with other titles within the entity. For example, for certain sustainability information, such activities may be performed by the compliance function or several different internal audit functions that exist within the entity (such as both an environmental, health, and safety internal audit function and a financial or operational internal audit function). Inquiries about the findings of relevant internal audit activities may be useful in planning the examination or review engagement to help identify any key risk areas. In considering whether the practitioner can use the work of such other function(s) as internal auditors, consistent with the requirements in AT-C section 205,[5] the practitioner should evaluate the level of competence, objectivity and to whom such other function(s) report, and whether each such other function has a systematic and disciplined approach, including quality control. Paragraphs 3.53–.55 provide guidance on using the work of internal auditors.

Measurement Uncertainty

2.23 A characteristic of certain sustainability information is that it cannot be measured with high accuracy. The degree of measurement uncertainty associated with such measurements could affect the risks of material misstatement of the subject matter, including the susceptibility of the subject matter to unintentional or intentional management bias. The extent of measurement uncertainty also may affect sustainability information users' ability to understand, use, and compare such information over time and between entities.

---

[5] Paragraphs .39–.44 of AT-C section 205.

2.24 In planning the engagement, relevant considerations include the following:

- *a.* Whether measurement uncertainty—the range of values that could reasonably be attributed to the reported point value—may be high in relation to any of the quantitative sustainability information subject to the attestation engagement, for purposes of
    - i. identifying risks of material misstatement in an examination engagement (see paragraphs 3.08E–.13) or
    - ii. placing an increased focus in areas of increased risk in a review engagement (see paragraphs 3.09R–.13)
- *b.* Whether management intends to include disclosures related to the reported point values with high measurement uncertainty, including disclosures about the source(s) of measurement uncertainty and a quantified expression of the measurement uncertainty, such as the range of values that could reasonably be attributed to the subject matter (refer to paragraph 1.19)

Using the Work of an Other Practitioner

2.25 In planning an engagement, practitioners also may consider whether they expect to use the work of an other practitioner (refer to paragraphs 1.51 and 5.33 for examples of situations in which the practitioner might use the work of an other practitioner with respect to sustainability information, including GHG emissions information). In determining whether to use the work of such other practitioner, the practitioner also should consider whether the same criteria were used for the measurement of the sustainability information examined or reviewed by the other practitioner as for the sustainability information subject to the practitioner's engagement and the standards of performance used by the other practitioner. As practitioners would need to perform additional procedures if different criteria or different performance standards were used, they may be less inclined to use the work of an other practitioner in such case.

2.26 Paragraph .31 of AT-C section 105, *Concepts Common to All Attestation Engagements*, includes requirements for when the practitioner expects to use the work of an other practitioner. If the practitioner expects to use the work of an other practitioner, the practitioner should establish an overall strategy and develop a plan for such use of the other practitioner's work, assessing the extent to which such work will be used and whether the practitioner intends to make reference to the report of the other practitioner.

2.27 When the practitioner is assuming responsibility for the work of an other practitioner, the practitioner should determine the type of work to be performed by the engagement team or by the other practitioner on the practitioner's behalf. The practitioner also should determine the nature, timing, and extent of its involvement in the work of the other practitioner.

Risk Assessment Procedures

2.28 Given some of the similarities in examination and review procedures, this guide presents the procedures to be performed in an examination and a review engagement in a columnar format when the procedures differ between an examination and a review, and in a standard paragraph format preceding

Planning the Examination or Review Engagement

or following the tables when the guidance is common to procedures for both forms of attestation engagements. Paragraphs in the tables relating to an examination only are numbered with an 'E,' while paragraphs relating strictly to a review are numbered with an 'R.' The topics of a particular row between the examination and review columns may not necessarily align with each other.

Examination	Review

2.29E AT-C section 205 requires, in an examination engagement, that the practitioner perform risk assessment procedures by obtaining an understanding of the following:[6]
    a. The subject matter and other engagement circumstances
    b. Internal control over the preparation of the subject matter relevant to the engagement, including evaluating the design of the controls and determining whether they have been implemented
	2.29R AT-C section 210 does not require the practitioner to perform risk assessment procedures in a review engagement nor obtain an understanding of internal control over the measurement, evaluation, or disclosure of the subject matter information in a review engagement. However, an understanding of relevant components of internal control over the measurement, evaluation, and disclosure of sustainability information may be helpful to appropriately plan the review engagement.

2.30E In the case of sustainability information, risk assessment procedures include obtaining an understanding of the processes and internal control over identifying, measuring, capturing, aggregating, retention, monitoring, and reporting of the sustainability information. As discussed in paragraph 2.18, the collection and reporting processes relating to sustainability information and internal control over those processes may not be fully developed, increasing the risk of material misstatement of the sustainability information.	**2.30R** Understanding the processes and internal control over identifying, measuring, capturing, aggregating, retention, monitoring, and reporting of the sustainability information may be helpful in identifying the nature and scope of the review procedures and the expected nature of review evidence. If documentation of the process is not available, the practitioner might perform inquiries and a walk-through of the process with the entity's management or other pertinent employees to gain an understanding of the process and systems used and the initial sources of capturing the data.

(continued)

---

[6] Paragraphs .14–.15 of AT-C section 205.

Examination	Review

2.31E Relevant matters to understand regarding internal control include the following components of the entity's internal control relevant to the sustainability information:
   a. The control environment.
   b. The entity's risk assessment process related to gathering, processing, retention, and reporting of sustainability information.
   c. Control activities relevant to the engagement. An attestation engagement does not require an understanding of all the control activities related to each significant measure (such as the sources of GHG emissions and disclosure in a schedule of GHG emissions information) or to every assertion relevant to them.
   d. The information system, including the related business processes, and communication of sustainability-reporting roles and responsibilities and significant matters relating to sustainability reporting.
   e. Monitoring activities.	

2.32 The practitioner's understanding of such relevant components of internal control might raise doubts in certain cases about whether the practitioner will be able to obtain sufficient evidence to complete the engagement. For example, an understanding of an entity's internal control might raise concerns about the condition and reliability of the entity's records, or cause the practitioner to question the reliability of management representations.

Materiality in Planning and Performing the Engagement

Examination	Review
2.33E As required by AT-C section 205, the practitioner should consider materiality for the subject matter when establishing the overall engagement strategy,[7] including the determination of the nature, timing, and extent of procedures; and when evaluating whether uncorrected misstatements are material—individually or in the aggregate.[8]	**2.33R** As required by AT-C section 210, the practitioner should consider materiality when planning and performing the review engagement, including the determination of the nature, timing, and extent of procedures; and when evaluating whether the practitioner is aware of any material modifications that should be made to the subject matter for it to be fairly presented in accordance with the criteria or the assertion in order for it to be fairly stated.[9]

2.34 Materiality as a concept relates to both (*a*) what information is material to users and thus should be included in the sustainability report, and (*b*) whether an identified misstatement, including an omitted disclosure, would be material to users.

2.35 Assessing the significance of a misstatement of some items of the sustainability information may be more dependent upon qualitative than quantitative considerations. Qualitative aspects of materiality relate to the relevance and reliability of the information presented (for example, qualitative aspects of materiality in assessing whether the underlying information, determinations, estimates, and assumptions of the entity provide a reasonable basis for the disclosures in the sustainability report). Furthermore, quantitative information is often more meaningful when accompanied by qualitative disclosures. For example, quantitative information about a measurement of GHG emissions may be more meaningful when accompanied by narrative regarding the source and extent of measurement uncertainty of such measurement.

2.36 When high measurement uncertainty exists, materiality considered in planning and performing the engagement may be smaller than the range of values reasonably attributed to such sustainability information. Information with complex measurement methods that incorporate multiple assumptions may result in high measurement uncertainty and, thus, a point value in that range may not be as accurate or precise for such sustainability information as information that can be easily counted or measured.

2.37 When measurement uncertainty is material to the engagement, the practitioner should design procedures that focus on obtaining evidence regarding the quality of the measurement process, whether there are any known errors, and whether the disclosures related to the reported information are sufficient.

---

[7] Paragraph .16 of AT-C section 205.
[8] Paragraph .59*b* of AT-C section 205.
[9] Paragraph .14 of AT-C section 210.

2.38 When the engagement is for an entire sustainability report, relevant materiality considerations may include

- obtaining an understanding of the process the entity's management undertook to identify what is material to the entity for sustainability reporting purposes;
- identification of the sustainability information that is most significant to the users of the report (material information); and
- determination of a threshold of materiality of misstatements for that information.

2.39 It is likely that the sustainability information considered most significant to users of the report will cover several different topics or indicators, in which case a materiality of misstatement threshold would be assessed for each such topic or indicator. Relevant factors to consider in identifying the sustainability information most significant to users of the report may include

- management's view on the materiality of the information;
- the materiality determination process that the entity undertakes to determine what information to include in the report; and
- the practitioner's understanding of the intended users.

2.40 When the engagement is to include only specified indicators, materiality is assessed for each such indicator. For example, if separate GHG emissions information is presented for Scopes 2 and 3 emissions, the practitioner might choose a materiality level based on the total of a particular scope, and perhaps select closer to the bottom of the range for the amount of *Scope 2 emissions* versus assessing materiality as a little higher in the range for *Scope 3 emissions*.

2.41 The types of misstatements that could occur in sustainability information include the following:

- Misstatement of quantified information (for example, understatement or overstatement of GHG emissions; omissions of activity for a period of time or a location; omission of the unit of measurement; or if the measurement uncertainty is high, the quantified extent of the measurement uncertainty)
- Misstatement of narrative (for example, not balanced or incomplete information, or inaccurate statement)
- Omitted disclosure (for example, lack of disclosure called for by the criteria or lack of a disclosure about a material event affecting the sustainability information)
- Insufficient description of the criteria (for example, for measurement of a particular indicator, the methodologies applied, measurement methods, assumptions, estimates, and factors used in making the measurement or evaluation might not be disclosed)

2.42 Relevant factors when evaluating whether an omission of a disclosure is material include whether the sustainability information is misleading in the context of the engagement without the needed disclosure (for example, whether the disclosures omit information needed to understand, compare, and use the sustainability information). Needed disclosures may be specified by the criteria or may be included in addition to that specified by the criteria (for example, disclosures that the practitioner deems necessary to achieve fair presentation).

2.43 Given the varied nature of sustainability information, for an engagement involving the entire sustainability report, the practitioner is likely to establish different materiality thresholds for evaluating misstatements of the different types of sustainability information considered material information (for example, GHG emissions versus labor statistics versus financial information). When the sustainability information is quantified, materiality of misstatements might be considered in terms of a percentage of such amount. If the sustainability information is narrative, materiality of misstatements might be considered in terms of qualitative factors in determining the overall engagement strategy or nature, timing, and extent of the procedures.

2.44 In some circumstances, the materiality of misstatements may be based on the criteria (for example, it might be stated in the criteria) and the intended use of such information (for example, when the materiality of a specified indicator is established by a regulator or other filing requirement).

Considerations When Selecting and Using the Work of a Practitioner's Specialist

2.45 AT-C section 205[10] includes requirements for when the practitioner expects to use the work of a practitioner's specialist in an examination engagement, and AT-C section 210[11] directs the practitioner to apply the requirement in AT-C section 205, as appropriate, for a review engagement. Considerations when selecting a practitioner's specialist include the following:

- The specialist's expertise and competence in the subject matter
- The relevance of the specialist's expertise to the practitioner's objectives in the attestation engagement
- The objectivity of the specialist
- The nature and extent of the anticipated use of the specialist

---

[10] Paragraphs .36–.38 of AT-C section 205.
[11] Paragraph .27 of AT-C section 210.

Chapter 3

Performing Examination or Review Procedures

3.01 Additional guidance specific to an attestation engagement on a separate presentation of greenhouse gas emissions (GHG) emissions information is included in chapter 5 and supplements the procedures contained in this chapter.

Examination	*Review*
Identifying Risks of Material Misstatement	**Placing an Increased Focus in Areas of Increased Risk**

3.02E Under AT-C section 205, *Examination Engagements*,[1] the practitioner is required to identify and assess risks of material misstatement as the basis for designing and performing further procedures whose nature, timing, and extent
 	
   a. are responsive to assessed risks of material misstatement and
 	
   b. allow the practitioner to obtain reasonable assurance about whether the sustainability information is presented in accordance with the criteria, in all material respects.[2]
	3.02R AT-C section 210, *Review Engagements*, requires the practitioner to place increased focus on areas in which the practitioner believes there are increased risks that the subject matter may be materially misstated.[3]

3.03E In the case of specified indicators, the risk of material misstatement is assessed in relation to each indicator. In the case of an identifiable section of a sustainability report, materiality and the risk of material misstatement are assessed in relation to that section. In an examination of an entire sustainability report, materiality and the risk of material misstatement are assessed in relation to the entire sustainability report.	**3.03R** In the case of specified indicators, the increased focus in areas of increased risk relates to each indicator. In the case of an identifiable section of a sustainability report, the increased focus in areas of increased risk relates to that section. In a review of an entire sustainability report, the increased focus in areas of increased risk relates to the entire sustainability report.

(continued)

---

[1] All AT-C sections in this guide can be found in AICPA *Professional Standards*.
[2] Paragraph .18 of AT-C section 205, *Examination Engagements*.
[3] Paragraph .18 of AT-C section 210, *Review Engagements*.

Examination	Review
3.04E Procedures performed in assessing risks of material misstatement can, among other procedures, include inquiries about the relationships of narrative statements to the sustainability metrics used and the source of the reported information. Inquiries about relationships of narrative statements to metrics used can identify inconsistencies or possible sources of evidence to support the disclosure, or corroborate the results of other inquiries.	**3.04R** Areas in which to place increased focus may be determined through inquiries about the reporting boundary, the relationships of narrative statements to the sustainability metrics used and the source of the reported information. Inquiries about relationships of narrative statements to metrics used can identify inconsistencies or possible sources of evidence to support the disclosure, or corroborate the results of other inquiries. The specific inquiries to be made are a function of the characteristics of the sustainability information, and the practitioner's knowledge of the industry in which the entity operates may be taken into consideration. (Refer to paragraph 3.17R)
3.05E The specific procedures to be performed are a function of the characteristics of the sustainability information and may take into consideration the following: • The industry in which the organization operates • The reporting boundary for purposes of the examination engagement and whether information to be reported is based on data received by the entity from organizations in the supply chain (see paragraphs 3.17E and 3.20E)	**3.05R** The nature of procedures in a review engagement concerning sustainability information will vary according to whether analytical procedures can be performed. Some sustainability information, although quantifiable in nature, may not be suitable for analytical procedures (for example, safety metrics). Analytical procedures may not be possible when the subject matter is qualitative rather than quantitative. AT-C section 210 states that, in these situations, the practitioner should perform other procedures, in addition to inquiries, that provide equivalent levels of review evidence[4] (such as inspection and observation). Paragraphs 3.34R–.35R discuss other review procedures.
3.06E In considering whether to perform analytical procedures, the practitioner should consider whether the information to which the analytical procedures would be applied is appropriate for analytical procedures. Some sustainability information, although quantifiable in nature, may not be suitable for analytical procedures. For example, the practitioner may be unable to obtain sufficient evidence for metrics, such as a health and safety statistic of fatalities per year, given the lack of a quantifiable relationship between the variables relating to such metric.	**3.06R** Even when there is the ability to perform analytical procedures, conditions may exist that might not produce a reliable basis on which to perform the procedures, or performing analytical procedures will be less effective and efficient than performing tests of details to obtain sufficient review evidence. For example, in obtaining review evidence related to an entity's community investment, it might be more effective to review documentary evidence of payments made or observe donated property in use.

---

[4] Paragraph .17 of AT-C section 210.

Measurement Uncertainty

3.07 Chapter 1, "Introduction to Sustainability Examination and Review Engagements," includes general guidance about measurement uncertainty. This section provides guidance on the procedures performed concerning measurement uncertainty in sustainability information. Although improved measurement techniques may reduce the range of measurement uncertainty, the underlying inherent uncertainty often cannot be further reduced or removed through more measurement or different techniques due to the nature of the sustainability information. Therefore, in those cases, examination or review procedures performed by the practitioner cannot reduce or remove the inherent uncertainty.

Examination	*Review*
3.08E The degree of measurement uncertainty associated with the reported information affects the identification and assessment of the risks of material misstatement in an examination of sustainability information and, accordingly, the practitioner should tailor further procedures to respond to the identified risks.	
3.09E When high measurement uncertainty is identified in sustainability information, the practitioner should evaluate whether, in the practitioner's professional judgment, the various aspects of the measurement process (for example, measurement techniques, assumptions, and conversion factors) gives rise to an increased risk of material misstatement.	**3.09R** When high measurement uncertainty is identified in sustainability information, the practitioner should place increased focus in those areas of measurement uncertainty arising from the various aspects of the measurement process (for example, measurement techniques, assumptions, and conversion factors) in which the practitioner believes there are increased risks that the sustainability information may be materially misstated.

3.10 Factors that may be considered when assessing whether the process resulting in high measurement uncertainty in sustainability information gives rise to an increased risk of material misstatement include the following:

- How reported values were measured (namely, the process used to arrive at the range of reasonable values)
- The source and extent of measurement uncertainty for reported point values included in the sustainability information
- How those reported point values were selected from within the range of reasonable values

- Whether other methods may be more or less accurate and precise[5] and why management intends to use the selected method
- Whether and what management intends to include as disclosures related to such reported point values, including disclosures about the source(s) of measurement uncertainty and a quantified expression of the measurement uncertainty, such as the range of values that could be reasonably attributed to the reported point values

3.11 Examples of measurements that might be identified as having high measurement uncertainty include the following:

- Those requiring high levels of judgment, for example, when significant assumptions could fall within a range of reasonable values that could significantly affect the measurement
- Those with a less accurate or less precise process for measuring the information
- Those that require the summation of multiple values, each with its own significant measurement uncertainty

3.12 Subject matter included in the scope of the engagement may extend beyond the organizational boundary of the reporting entity and its subsidiaries to include information from noncontrolled entities such as vendors, suppliers, and intermediaries. The reporting entity's ability to obtain accurate information from those noncontrolled entities may be limited and alternative, less accurate, or less precise means may be employed to estimate the sustainability information applicable to such entities (for example, estimating the measurement using factors applied to information in the entity's possession rather than more accurate or more precise measurements at the noncontrolled entity).

3.13 When there is high measurement uncertainty involved in quantitative measurements included in a sustainability report, presenting such measurements as a range or including other types of disclosures quantifying the measurement uncertainty may assist users of the report in understanding the variability of the measurement and in making comparisons between periods and entities. Taking planned disclosures into consideration in designing the procedures to be performed assists in identifying sufficient engagement evidence to be obtained.

---

[5] Refer to the footnote to paragraph 1.14 regarding the use in this guide of the technical definitions for *accuracy* and *precision* that are common for engineers and scientists.

Responding to Assessed Risks and Obtaining Evidence

Examination	Review
3.14E In accordance with AT-C section 205, the practitioner is required to • obtain sufficient appropriate evidence to reduce attestation risk to an acceptably low level and thereby enable the practitioner to draw reasonable conclusions on which to base the practitioner's opinion on the sustainability information, and • design and implement overall responses to address the assessed risks of material misstatement in the sustainability information.[6]	**3.14R** In accordance with AT-C section 210, the practitioner should design and perform analytical procedures and make inquiries and perform other procedures, as appropriate, to accumulate review evidence in obtaining limited assurance about whether any material modifications should be made to the sustainability information in order for it to be in accordance with the criteria, or the assertion in order for it to be fairly stated.[7]
3.15E The evidence required to support the level of assurance obtained is a matter of professional judgment. AT-C section 205 provides guidance about the evidence to be obtained in an examination engagement; evidence is considered regardless of whether it appears to corroborate or contradict the measurement or evaluation of the subject matter or assertion. Types and examples of evidence that the practitioner may consider obtaining in an examination of sustainability information include the following: • Evidence of the completeness and accuracy of amounts disclosed, including how the sustainability information has been calculated and the underlying methodologies applied, measurement methods, assumptions, estimates, and conversion factors used in making the measurement or evaluation (see paragraph 3.16) • Evidence regarding the reasonableness of narrative statements (for example, communications within the entity regarding the entity's targets for the subsequent period)	**3.15R** The evidence required to support the level of assurance obtained is a matter of professional judgment. AT-C section 210 provides guidance about the evidence to be obtained in review engagements; review evidence is considered regardless of whether it appears to corroborate or contradict the measurement or evaluation of the subject matter or assertion. Types and examples of review evidence that the practitioner may consider obtaining in a review of sustainability information include the following: • Evidence regarding the reasonableness of amounts disclosed, including regarding the reasonableness of the basis of measurement (for example, how the sustainability information has been calculated, and the underlying methodologies, measurement methods, assumptions, estimates, and conversion factors used in making the measurement or evaluation [see paragraph 3.16]) • Evidence regarding the reasonableness of narrative statements (for example, communications within the entity regarding the entity's targets for the subsequent period)

---

[6] Paragraphs .19–.20 of AT-C section 205.
[7] Paragraph .16 of AT-C section 210.

3.16 Evidence regarding the completeness and accuracy (in an examination) or reasonableness (in a review) of amounts disclosed, including how the sustainability information has been calculated, may be obtained from a variety of sources, including from supporting schedules, such as the following:

- Detailed schedules aggregated and maintained by the entity's sustainability reporting department. Characteristics for the practitioner to look for include whether the aggregation of data in these schedules follows the criteria adopted and disclosed by the entity and covers the entire reporting boundary. For example, the data may be supported by a monthly invoice from the supplier (such as for electricity or water usage), or an invoice that has been allocated based on an acceptable method of estimating (such as square footage, head count, units of production).
- Detailed schedules collected and maintained through the entity's existing system of processes and controls for regulatory or compliance matters (for example, incident reports).
- Supporting schedules of detail from third parties such as electricity invoices for all, or a subset of, facilities; air travel details provided by the entity's travel administrator.

If using information produced by the entity, refer to paragraphs 3.49E–.52E in an examination engagement or paragraph 3.49R in a review engagement.

Examination	Review
Reporting Boundary	**Reporting Boundary**

3.17E Relevant procedures with respect to the reporting boundary include obtaining evidence in connection with the risk assessment procedures as to the following:
 	
• Whether the reporting boundary is consistent with that used in the prior period.
• Whether the information reported is based on data supplied to the entity by organizations in the supply chain (see paragraph 3.05E). If so, procedures such as the following might be performed on such data for purposes of obtaining evidence to evaluate the appropriateness of including such information:
  — Confirming the information with the party that supplied it to the entity, including whether such information is accurate and complete
  — Comparing such information with industry statistics or other publicly reported information by other organizations
  — Considering the consistency of such external information with internal information of the entity
 	
Also, refer to paragraph 3.20E regarding third-party information.
	3.17R Relevant procedures with respect to the reporting boundary include the following:
	
	• Inquiring as to whether the reporting boundary used for the sustainability information is consistent with that of prior periods
	• Considering whether information to be reported is based on data received by the entity from organizations in the supply chain
	• Evaluating the appropriateness of the planned procedures in light of the reporting boundary for purposes of the review engagement (refer to paragraph 3.04R)

Procedures

Examination	Review
Further Procedures	**Analytical Procedures**

3.18E AT-C section 205 requires the practitioner to design and perform further procedures whose nature, timing and extent are based on, and responsive to, the assessed risks of material misstatement.[8] The practitioner may perform analytical procedures in response to assessed risks.	**3.18R** When designing and performing analytical procedures, AT-C section 210 states that the practitioner should
	
	   a. determine the suitability of particular analytical procedures for the subject matter, taking account of the practitioner's awareness of risks.
	
	   b. evaluate the reliability of data from which the practitioner's expectation is developed, taking into account the source, comparability, nature, and relevance of information available.
	
	   c. develop an expectation with respect to recorded amounts or ratios.[9]
	
	Paragraphs 3.24–.26 provide guidance on certain considerations regarding analytical procedures.

(continued)

---

[8] Paragraph .21 of AT-C section 205.
[9] Paragraph .19 of AT-C section 210.

Examination	Review

3.19E When designing and performing analytical procedures in response to assessed risk, AT-C section 205 states that the practitioner should
    a. determine the suitability of particular analytical procedures for the subject matter, taking into account the assessed risks of material misstatement and any related tests of details.
    b. evaluate the reliability of data from which the practitioner's expectation is developed, taking into account the source, comparability, nature, and relevance of information available, and controls over their preparation (also see paragraph 3.50E).
    c. develop an expectation that is sufficiently precise to identify possible material misstatements (taking into account whether analytical procedures are to be performed alone or in combination with tests of details).[10]
	3.19R To perform the analytical procedures, the practitioner may obtain the report or analysis prepared by the entity with respect to each material sustainability metric and may make inquiries about the source of the information, the assumptions used and any related qualitative disclosures. The reliability of the data might be considered using the factors described in paragraph 3.50E.

3.20E The practitioner performs procedures in an examination to obtain evidence concerning the completeness and accuracy of measurements, including the disclosure of measurement uncertainty. Such procedures may involve considerations concerning the use of third-party services and the availability of third-party information. Examples of procedures concerning third-party information include the following:
 	
• Consideration of the source of the third-party information
• Understanding the processes and assumptions used by the third party and whether the third party obtained assurance over its processes
• Consideration of the control environment at the third party
• Other procedures to assess the reliability of such information
	Inquiries
	
	3.20R AT-C section 210 states that the practitioner should inquire of the responsible party concerning the following:
	    a. Whether the subject matter has been prepared in accordance with the criteria (refer to paragraph 3.27)
	    b. The practices used by the responsible party to measure, recognize, and record the subject matter (refer to paragraph 3.28)
	    c. Questions that have arisen in the course of applying the review procedures (refer to paragraph 3.21R)
	    d. Communications from regulatory agencies or others, if relevant[11] (refer to paragraph 3.22R)

---

[10] Paragraph .27 of AT-C section 205.
[11] Paragraph .21 of AT-C section 210.

Performing Examination or Review Procedures

Examination	Review

3.21E Further procedures concerning quantitative sustainability information may include the following:
 	
- Tracing data to its source
- Examining relevant contracts or confirming details of the transactions with other parties
- Testing completeness by considering other sources of evidence and tracing back to the sustainability information to ascertain whether it has been properly included
- Ascertaining whether conversion factors have been properly applied, whether the underlying assumptions have been documented and whether those assumptions have a reasonable basis (for example, if industry standards are used, establishing the source, reliability and whether the most up-to-date factors have been used)
- Ascertaining whether there have been any changes in the criteria or factors used to calculate the sustainability information; when applicable, ascertaining whether component entities have used the same criteria or factors
- Conducting site visits for significant locations
- Making inquiries of entity personnel about the following and obtaining evidence to evaluate explanations regarding any such matters:
  — Whether there have been any changes in operations (for example, lower production levels because of a long-term outage; changes in base years, such as changes resulting from the sale or acquisition of operational facilities or subsidiaries)
  — The nature of significant judgments and estimates made by management and any uncertainties regarding measurements
  — Whether there have been any communications from regulators concerning noncompliance with *permits* or regulatory schemes
	3.21R Questions may arise if the practitioner notes any of the following types of matters in the course of applying the review procedures and the practitioner may seek to obtain further information by making inquiries of management of the responsible party about such matter(s):
	
	- A potential error (for example, a misalignment with the criteria, a supporting schedule that does not align with the disclosure)
	- An omission (for example, exclusion of measurements for a period of time or location; lack of a significant disclosure)
	- An inconsistency (for example, the use of multiple methods of measurement, multiple conversion factors, or different methods for different locations)

(continued)

Examination	Review
• Performing cutoff procedures to assess whether transactions at both the beginning and end of the period have, as appropriate, been included in or excluded from the reported information • Comparing the reported sustainability information to the underlying records and checking the mathematical accuracy thereof • Testing significant reconciliations and examining significant reconciling items • Examining material adjustments made during the course of preparing the sustainability information • Requesting a legal letter (for example, to address noncompliance with laws or regulations, noncompliance with GHG emissions regulatory schemes, or threatened litigation related to hazardous waste, employee related health and safety matters, or ownership matters) • Obtaining and reading internal audit reports and minutes of audit committee meetings (or other relevant board committees to which the internal auditors report on sustainability information)	
3.22E Further procedures concerning qualitative disclosures may include inquiries and other procedures related to the assumptions used, such as the following: • Considering who to make additional inquiries of and the documents that might exist relating to such matters • Reading board minutes • Obtaining analyses performed by management and relevant documents	**3.22R** Questions concerning communications from regulatory agencies or others might include whether there have been any communications from regulatory agencies concerning noncompliance with permits or regulatory schemes. Consideration may also be given to requesting a legal letter when considered appropriate (for example, to address noncompliance with regulatory schemes, or threatened litigation related to hazardous waste, employee related health and safety matters, or ownership matters).
3.23E Certain procedures may be performed as "dual-purpose" testing in conjunction with the testing of the operating effectiveness of relevant controls discussed in paragraph 3.33E.	

Considerations Regarding Analytical Procedures

3.24 Inquiries and analytical procedures are often interrelated. For example, responses to inquiries about whether there have been any changes in operations, such as lower production levels because of a long-term outage, or changes in base years, such as sales or acquisitions of operational facilities or subsidiaries, may help the practitioner develop appropriate expectations for related analytical procedures.

3.25 The practitioner might identify external information that can be used to evaluate the reliability of data included in the analysis or to develop an expectation. For example, (*a*) miles traveled might be obtained from an external travel agent to compare to the information reflected in the entity's analysis or to develop an expectation regarding greenhouse gas emissions related to travel or (*b*) utility bills might be used to recalculate GHG emissions or to perform other analytical procedures. AT-C section 210 does not require the practitioner to evaluate the reliability of information produced by the entity in a review engagement (see paragraph 3.49R).

3.26 In evaluating the responses to the practitioner's inquiries, considerations might include the consistency of the responses with the practitioner's understanding of the business, knowledge of the industry in which the entity operates and the results of other procedures performed.

Inquiries About the Subject Matter

3.27 Inquiries of the responsible party about whether the subject matter has been prepared in accordance with the criteria include inquiries that assist the practitioner in the following:

- Understanding why specified indicators and measurement criteria were selected
- Understanding whether the criteria were customized or interpreted and, if so, how the criteria were customized or interpreted and whether the customized or interpreted criteria are objective (unbiased)
- Ascertaining whether management has elected to report only favorable indicators or use more favorable measurement criteria

3.28 Examples of inquiries about the practices used by the responsible party to measure, recognize, and record the subject matter include inquiries about the following:

- The measurement tools and methodology used, alternative methodologies that might have been used and the reasons for the selected approach
- The appropriateness of the reported point estimate selected in relation to (*a*) the range of probable values and (*b*) the distribution of values within the range, and how and why the reported point values were selected in this and prior periods
- The nature of significant judgments and estimates made by management and any uncertainties regarding measurements, including the quantified expression of measurement uncertainty
- The consistency of the criteria or measurement methods used with the prior period (see paragraphs 3.68E–.73 for examination engagements and paragraphs 3.68R–.73 for review engagements)

- Cutoff procedures performed at both the period beginning and period end
- Whether and the extent to which activities of internal audit encompassed the sustainability information

General Inquiry Considerations

3.29 Inquiries may be made of one individual; however, it is often useful to make the same or similar inquiries of others to corroborate such responses. Knowledge gained in obtaining an understanding of the entity during planning and other procedures is relevant in considering the responses received and in determining whether other procedures are to be performed.

3.30 The consistency of the responses with the practitioner's understanding of the business, knowledge of the industry in which the entity operates and the results of other procedures performed are relevant matters in evaluating the responses to the practitioner's inquiries.

Tests of Controls

Examination	*Review*
3.31E In accordance with AT-C section 205, the practitioner is required to design and perform tests of controls to obtain sufficient appropriate evidence about the operating effectiveness of relevant controls if (*a*) the practitioner intends to rely on the operating effectiveness of controls in determining the nature, timing, and extent of other procedures; or (*b*) procedures other than tests of controls cannot alone provide sufficient appropriate evidence.[12] Paragraph .25 of AT-C section 205 also includes requirements for addressing identified deviations in the controls.	**3.31R** Tests of controls are not performed; however, see paragraphs 2.29R–.30R and 2.32 regarding obtaining an understanding of the processes and internal control over identifying, measuring, capturing, aggregating, monitoring and reporting of the sustainability information.
3.32E As described in paragraph 2.18, the collection and reporting processes and controls may not be fully developed. Accordingly, a control reliance strategy might not be possible.	

---

[12] Paragraph .24*a*–*b* of AT-C section 205.

Performing Examination or Review Procedures

Examination	Review
3.33E When it is possible to test controls over the sustainability information, with respect to estimates and other measurements that are material information, it is generally appropriate to test the operating effectiveness of the controls. Factors to consider may include • the source and flow of data into the measurement process; • the selection and modification of measurement methods and processes; • the management, evaluation and disclosure of measurement uncertainty; and • the selection of the specific value reported.	

Procedures Other Than Tests of Controls

Examination	Review
3.34E As required by AT-C section 205, irrespective of the assessed risks of material misstatement, the practitioner should design and perform tests of details or analytical procedures related to the sustainability information.[13] Data analytics may be useful in performing tests of details, analytical procedures, or tests of details in combination with analytical procedures.	**Other Review Procedures** **3.34R** In circumstances in which inquiry and analytical procedures are not expected to provide sufficient appropriate review evidence, or when the nature of the subject matter does not lend itself to the application of analytical procedures, the practitioner may perform other procedures that he or she believes can provide the practitioner with a level of assurance equivalent to that which inquiries and analytical procedures would have provided.

(continued)

---

[13] Paragraph .26 of AT-C section 205.

Examination	Review
3.35E Even when the practitioner is able to form an expectation relating to the sustainability information and to perform analytical procedures, the processes in place to record and report the sustainability information need to be sufficient to produce a reliable basis on which to perform the procedures. The lower the reliance on internal control, the more likely it is the practitioner would perform tests of details.	**3.35R** Examples of other review procedures include the following: • Conducting site visits for significant locations for purposes of inquiry and understanding the business and access to pertinent records • Observation of evidence of thoroughness of data collection process • Performing data analytics to obtain review evidence • Comparisons of the reported sustainability information to the underlying records • Performing tests of mathematical accuracy of computations • Performing tests of significant analyses or reconciliations prepared by the entity in developing the sustainability information, including material adjustments made during the course of preparing the sustainability information • Consideration of other information of which the practitioner becomes aware and its implications on the sustainability information • Reading relevant contracts to understand terms related to relevant sustainability information or to corroborate a response to an inquiry

Performing Examination or Review Procedures

Examination	Review
3.36E In some situations, for reasons beyond a difficulty in forming an expectation relating to the sustainability information, performing analytical procedures will be less effective and efficient than performing tests of details to obtain evidence. For example, in obtaining evidence related to an entity's community investment, it might be more effective and efficient to confirm significant donations with beneficiaries, compare significant contributions to check copies and bank statements, or observe donated property in use. For other metrics, such as health and safety statistics of injuries per year, the qualitative significance of presenting an accurate number could also result in tests of details being more effective than an analytical procedure.	

Procedures Regarding Estimates and Measurement Uncertainty

Examination	Review
3.37E AT-C section 205 requires the practitioner to evaluate, based on the assessed risks of material misstatement, whether (*a*) the responsible party has appropriately applied the requirements of the criteria relevant to any estimated amounts and (*b*) the methods for making estimates are appropriate and have been applied consistently, and whether changes, if any, in reported estimates or in the method for making them from the prior period, if applicable, are appropriate in the circumstances.[14]	

(continued)

---

[14] Paragraph .29 of AT-C section 205.

Examination	Review

3.38E AT-C section 205 also requires the practitioner to undertake one or more of the following when responding to an assessed risk of material misstatement related to an estimate, taking into account the nature of the estimate:
   a. Determine whether events occurring up to the date of the practitioner's report provide evidence regarding the estimate.
   b. Test how the responsible party made the estimate and the data on which it is based. In doing so, the practitioner should evaluate whether the
      i. method of measurement used is appropriate in the circumstances,
      ii. assumptions used by the responsible party are reasonable, and
      iii. data on which the estimate is based are sufficiently reliable for the practitioner's purposes.
   c. Test the operating effectiveness of the controls over how the responsible party made the estimate, together with other appropriate further procedures.
   d. Develop a point estimate or a range to evaluate the responsible party's estimate taking into consideration the following:
      i. If the practitioner uses assumptions or methods that differ from those of the responsible party, the practitioner should obtain an understanding of the responsible party's assumptions or methods sufficient to establish that the practitioner's point estimate or range takes into account relevant variables and to evaluate any significant differences from the responsible party's point estimate.
      ii. If the practitioner concludes that it is appropriate to use a range, the practitioner should narrow the range, based on evidence available, until all outcomes within the range are considered reasonable.[15]	

---

[15] Paragraph .30 of AT-C section 205.

Examination	Review

3.39E When examining estimates and other measurements, relevant considerations may include evaluating whether the methods for making estimates and other measurements are appropriate and have been applied consistently, and whether changes, if any, in reported measurements or in the method for making them from the prior period, if applicable, are appropriate in the circumstances. When there is a significant change in the methodology used to make a material measurement, relevant matters that the practitioner may evaluate include whether
 	
    a. the disclosures related to the change are appropriate, and
    b. the entity has justified that the alternative is preferable.
	3.39R When reviewing estimates and other measurements, inquiries by the practitioner may include the following:
	
	    a. Whether the methods for making estimates and other measurements are appropriate and have been applied consistently
	    b. Whether changes, if any, in reported measurements or in the method for making them from the prior period, if applicable, are appropriate in the circumstances. When there is a significant change in the methodology used to make a material measurement, such inquiries also may include the following:
	        i. Whether the disclosures related to the change are appropriate
	        ii. Whether the entity has justified that the alternative is preferable
	    c. Whether significant assumptions are reasonable
	    d. Whether the data on which the measurement is based is sufficiently reliable for the practitioner's purposes

(continued)

Examination	Review
3.40E When examining measurements, including estimates, relevant procedures that the practitioner may perform include the following: • Obtaining an understanding of how the quantified measurement uncertainty to be disclosed was determined and evaluating whether the determination reflects significant sources of measurement uncertainty and the total has been appropriately accumulated. • Testing the computation or other determination of the quantified measurement uncertainty to be disclosed and evaluating whether the measurement method, significant assumptions, and confidence level[16] on which the disclosed quantified measurement uncertainty is based is reasonable and consistent with prior periods. • Evaluating the appropriateness of the point value selected for disclosure in relation to (*a*) the range of probable values and (*b*) the distribution of values within the range. This evaluation includes understanding management's efforts to address measurement uncertainty and whether indicators of management bias exist in making the measurement or selecting the reported point value. For example, for an expected normal distribution of	**3.40R** In performing a review of a material matter with high measurement uncertainty, relevant procedures that the practitioner may perform include the following: • Considering whether to make inquiries about the operating effectiveness of the controls over how the responsible party made the measurement and developed disclosures—specifically, the controls over the source and flow of data into the measurement process; controls over the selection and modification of measurement methods and processes; controls over the management, evaluation and disclosure of measurement uncertainty; and controls over the selection of the specific point value reported. • Inquiring about how the quantified measurement uncertainty to be disclosed was determined, whether it reflects significant sources of measurement uncertainty and how the responsible party determined that the total has been appropriately accumulated. • Inquiring about whether the measurement method, significant assumptions, and confidence level[17] on which the disclosed quantified measurement uncertainty is based is reasonable and consistent with prior periods.

---

[16] As noted in paragraph 1.19, to be useful, the disclosed range of measurement uncertainty would include all reasonable outcomes, but not all possible outcomes. The confidence level associated with reasonable outcomes will vary depending on the subject matter, but generally will be lower than confidence levels associated with high or moderate assurance for sampling purposes (see paragraph 3.42 of AICPA Audit Guide *Audit Sampling*).

[17] As noted in paragraph 1.19, to be useful, the disclosed range of measurement uncertainty would include all reasonable outcomes, but not all possible outcomes. The confidence level associated with reasonable outcomes will vary depending on the subject matter, but generally will be lower than confidence levels associated with high or moderate assurance for sampling purposes (see paragraph 3.42 of AICPA Audit Guide *Audit Sampling*).

Examination	Review
values, the selected point value is generally near the midpoint of the range, but for a distribution that is skewed, the selected point value is generally near the value with the highest probability or the mathematically determined "expected" value. In other cases, the distribution may not have a point reasonably representative of the highest probability and consultation with a measurement specialist may be needed to evaluate whether the point value selected by management is appropriately representational of the measured subject matter. • Evaluating the consistency of the selection of the reported point value from period to period and the basis for any change in the rationale for the selection of the reported point value. For example, when the point value selected has changed from the prior period based on a subjective assessment that there has been a change in circumstances, the change could be arbitrary or an indicator of possible management bias. • Evaluating whether the planned disclosure of the source(s) of measurement uncertainty and the quantified expression of measurement uncertainty are understandable, comparable, useful and not misleading, considering the materiality of the reported information.	• Inquiring about the appropriateness of the point value selected for disclosure in relation to the following: — The range of probable values. — The distribution of values within the range. Such inquiries are directed to obtaining an understanding of management's efforts to address measurement uncertainty and whether indicators of management bias may exist in making the measurement or selecting the reported point value. For example, for an expected normal distribution of values, the selected point value is generally near the midpoint of the range, but for a distribution that is skewed, the selected point value is generally near the value with the highest probability or the mathematically determined "expected" value. In other cases, the distribution may not have a point reasonably representative of the highest probability and consultation with a measurement specialist may be needed to evaluate whether the point value selected by the responsible party is appropriately representational of the measured subject matter.

(continued)

Examination	Review
	• Inquiring about the consistency of the selection of the reported point value from period to period and the basis for any change in the rationale for the selection of the reported point value. For example, when the point value selected has changed from the prior period based on a subjective assessment that there has been a change in circumstances, the change could be arbitrary or an indicator of possible management bias. • Considering whether the planned disclosure of the sources of measurement uncertainty and the quantified expression of measurement uncertainty are understandable, comparable, useful, and not misleading, considering the materiality of the reported information.

Sampling

Examination	Review
3.41E If sampling is used, AT-C section 205 requires the practitioner to, when designing the sample, consider the purpose of the procedure and the characteristics of the population from which the sample will be drawn.[18]	

---

[18] Paragraph .31 of AT-C section 205.

Examination	Review
3.42E If the entity's systems, processes, and controls are expected to produce reliable information that can therefore be tested on a sample basis, sampling might be used in an examination of sustainability information to select items to be tested for purposes of, for example, • comparing monthly electricity or water usage to an invoice from the supplier or • observing an employee's electronic signoff of the entity's code of conduct.	
3.43E As discussed in paragraphs 1.29–.30, a common concern with sustainability information is the completeness of the population being tested. This risk would not be addressed by increasing the desired level of assurance via a larger sample size (that is, testing more of a potentially incomplete population does not provide evidence of completeness). Rather, completeness is typically addressed by procedures focused specifically on the completeness assertion (for example, reconciliation, accounting for the numerical sequence of transactions, accounting for all locations within the reporting boundary).	

Fraud, Laws, and Regulations

Examination	Review
3.44E AT-C section 205 states that the practitioner should a. consider whether risk assessment procedures and other procedures related to understanding the subject matter indicate risk of material misstatement due to fraud or noncompliance with laws or regulations. b. make inquiries of appropriate parties to determine whether they have knowledge of any actual, suspected, or alleged fraud or noncompliance with laws or regulations affecting the subject matter. c. evaluate whether there are unusual or unexpected relationships within the subject matter, or between the subject matter and other related information, that indicate risks of material misstatement due to fraud or noncompliance with laws or regulations. d. evaluate whether other information obtained indicates risk of material misstatement due to fraud or noncompliance with laws or regulations.[19]	**3.44R** AT-C section 210 requires the practitioner to (1) make inquiries of appropriate parties to determine whether they have knowledge of any actual, suspected, or alleged fraud or noncompliance with laws or regulations affecting the subject matter and (2) respond appropriately to fraud or suspected fraud and noncompliance or suspected noncompliance with laws or regulations affecting the subject matter that is identified during the engagement.[20]

3.45 The reporting of sustainability information is a less developed area than financial reporting: Controls may be immature, governance can be variable, and measurement and reporting standards are less harmonized. All these factors heighten the risk of intentional misstatement, including fraud—particularly where there are pressures to conform to targets, whether set by external parties such as regulators and customers, or by the entity as a performance incentive. Examples of misstatements or fraudulent activities that could occur include the following:

- Misstating the base line to make reported sustainability information look more favorable in subsequent periods
- Falsifying records (for example, in a greenhouse gas emissions context, to overstate carbon *credits* generated by the project)

---

[19] Paragraph .32 of AT-C section 205.
[20] Paragraphs .23–.24 of AT-C section 210.

Performing Examination or Review Procedures

- Understating health and safety incidents or work-related illnesses
- Destroying or excluding negative results of surveys (for example, employee or customer surveys, factory inspections) and only presenting favorable results
- Bribing officials to facilitate approvals or secure rights in developing countries, or to minimize fines or avoid negative publicity
- Misstating compliance metrics that may be associated with penalties or fines
- Misstating metrics associated with aggressive internal or external goals
- Misstating metrics linked to product or corporate public statements or claims
- Misstating metrics linked to performance and compensation
- Misstating metrics associated with specific project milestones, budget approval, rights to access certain markets or begin projects in certain markets or geographies

Revision of Risk Assessment

Examination	*Review*
3.46E AT-C section 205 requires the practitioner to revise the assessment and modify the planned procedures accordingly in circumstances in which the practitioner obtains evidence from performing further procedures, or if new information is obtained, either of which is inconsistent with the evidence on which the practitioner originally based the assessment.[21]	**3.46R** AT-C section 210 states that if the practitioner believes the subject matter may be materially misstated, the practitioner should perform additional procedures sufficient to obtain limited assurance about whether any material modifications should be made to the subject matter in order for it to be in accordance with the criteria or the assertion in order for it to be fairly stated.[22]

(continued)

---

[21] Paragraph .34 of AT-C section 205.
[22] Paragraph .26 of AT-C section 210.

Examination	Review
3.47E During the engagement, the practitioner may become aware of situations in which the sustainability information was not collected, measured, or reported in accordance with the expected process, or that there were misstatements in the process due to error or fraud. Examples include the following: • Errors were observed when comparing data with a source document (for example, kilowatt hours [kwh] used or miles traveled per a spreadsheet do not agree to the invoice). • Matters arose from tests of key reconciliations that may be indicative of increased fraud risks or control deficiencies with wider assurance implications. • Additional sources of the subject matter were observed (for example, GHG emissions from a machine not included in the inventory). • Locations throughout the entity and other entities within the reporting boundary were using different estimation methods, factors, or methodologies to develop the sustainability information. • Results were improperly adjusted due to pressure to achieve a metric which served as an input into an incentive compensation calculation.	
3.48E When such situations are encountered, relevant considerations may include the following: • Discussing the matter with management and the audit committee • Evaluating whether the engagement should be suspended while management, the internal audit function or external parties investigate • Extending procedures performed to gather evidence	

Evaluating the Reliability of Information Produced by the Entity

Examination	*Review*
3.49E When using information produced by the entity, AT-C section 205 requires the practitioner to evaluate whether the information is sufficiently reliable for the practitioner's purposes.[23]	**3.49R** AT-C section 210 does not require the practitioner to evaluate the reliability of information produced by the entity. However, if the practitioner becomes aware that information coming to the practitioner's attention is incorrect, incomplete, or unsatisfactory, the practitioner is required to request that the responsible party consider the effect of these matters on the subject matter and communicate the results of its consideration to the practitioner. This may cause the practitioner to perform additional procedures sufficient to obtain limited assurance.[24]
3.50E Relevant factors to consider in assessing the reliability of data produced by the entity may include the following: • Whether the data can be traced back to a source and, where applicable, details of the transactions confirmed • Whether the data was developed under a process with effective controls, including review • Whether the data is obtained from independent sources outside the entity or from within the entity • Whether the sources within the entity were independent of those who are responsible for the data and the review of such data	

(continued)

---

[23] Paragraph .35 of AT-C section 205.
[24] Paragraphs .25–.26 of AT-C section 210.

Examination	Review

3.51E If information to be used as evidence has been prepared using the work of a *management's specialist*, the practitioner should, to the extent necessary, taking into account the significance of that specialist's work for the practitioner's purposes,
    a. evaluate the competence, capabilities, and objectivity of that specialist;
    b. obtain an understanding of the work of that specialist; and
    c. evaluate the appropriateness of that specialist's work as evidence for the examination.	

3.52E If the entity uses a third-party data collection or data consolidation tool, the practitioner should consider what steps management has taken to determine that the tool is appropriate for the entity's purposes (for example, tools and spreadsheets to calculate GHG emissions).	

Using the Work of a Practitioner's Specialist or Internal Auditors

Examination	Review
3.53E When the practitioner expects to use the work of a practitioner's specialist or internal auditors in an examination engagement relating to sustainability information, the practitioner should apply the requirements in AT-C section 205, and the related application guidance, for an examination engagement.	**3.53R** AT-C section 210 states that when the practitioner expects to use the work of a practitioner's specialist or internal auditors in a review engagement, the practitioner should apply the requirements in AT-C section 205 and related application guidance, as appropriate for a review engagement.[25]

---

[25] Paragraph .27 of AT-C section 210.

Performing Examination or Review Procedures

3.54E The practitioner might use the work of a practitioner's specialist in an examination engagement relating to sustainability information to provide specialized skill or knowledge in a particular field other than accounting or auditing. For example, the entity may include information concerning the following: • GHG emissions, which might involve a scientist or an engineer • Water data, which might involve a water specialist • Health and safety matters, which might involve a safety engineer or labor law specialist Similarly, the practitioner might involve a practitioner's specialist to evaluate the work performed by the responsible party or management's specialist.	**3.54R** Paragraphs 3.53E and 3.54E describe the manner in which a practitioner's specialist might be used in an examination engagement related to sustainability information. A practitioner's specialist might also be used in a similar manner in a review engagement; however, the extent of review evidence to be obtained might be less.

3.55 Internal auditors may have performed work regarding the entity's sustainability performance or concerning compliance of the entity with requirements of specified laws, regulations, rules, contracts, or grants that might be pertinent to the sustainability information reported. Accordingly, the practitioner might use such work to obtain evidence regarding the sustainability information, or the practitioner might also use internal auditors to provide direct assistance as discussed in paragraphs .39–.43 of AT-C section 205 for an examination engagement (for example, internal audit may be used to assist in examining source documents and performing recalculations). Although AT-C section 210 does not address direct assistance in a review engagement, there may be circumstances in which the practitioner might consider using internal auditors to provide direct assistance in a review engagement (for example, internal auditors might be used to perform a detailed analysis of monthly changes for a particular sustainability indicator to enable the practitioner to inquire as to the causes of such fluctuations).

Using the Work of an Other Practitioner

3.56 When using the work of an other practitioner, regardless of whether the practitioner intends to make reference to the work of the other practitioner, the practitioner should evaluate whether the other practitioner's work is adequate for the practitioner's purposes. In doing so, the practitioner would read the sustainability information and the other practitioner's report to identify significant findings and issues and, when considered necessary, communicate with the other practitioner in this regard.

Evaluating the Results of Examination or Review Procedures

Examination	Review
3.57E In evaluating the results of examination procedures, AT-C section 205 requires the practitioner to a. accumulate misstatements identified during the engagement, other than those that are clearly trivial, and b. evaluate the sufficiency and appropriateness of the evidence obtained in the context of the engagement and, if necessary, attempt to obtain further evidence.[26]	**3.57R** In evaluating the results of review procedures, AT-C section 210 requires the practitioner to a. accumulate misstatements identified during the engagement, other than those that are clearly trivial, and b. evaluate the sufficiency and appropriateness of the review evidence obtained in the context of the engagement and, if necessary, attempt to obtain further review evidence.[27]
3.58E In accordance with AT-C section 205, uncorrected misstatements are accumulated during the engagement for the purpose of evaluating whether, individually or in aggregate, they are material when forming the practitioner's opinion.[28]	

3.59 The types of misstatements that could occur in sustainability information include the following:

- Misstatement of quantified information (for example, understatement or overstatement of GHG emissions, omissions of activity for a period of time or a location, omission of the unit of measurement, or if high measurement uncertainty exists, the omission or misstatement of the quantified extent of the measurement uncertainty)

- Misstatement of narrative (for example, lack of balanced disclosure, incomplete information or inaccurate statement)

- Omitted disclosure (for example, lack of a disclosure called for by the specified reporting criteria or lack of a disclosure about a material event affecting the sustainability information)

- Insufficient description of the criteria (for example, for measurement of a particular indicator or interpretations of criteria)

---

[26] Paragraphs .45–.46 of AT-C section 205.
[27] Paragraphs .28–.29 of AT-C section 210.
[28] Paragraph .A47 of AT-C section 205.

Performing Examination or Review Procedures

3.60 The manner in which such misstatements of sustainability information are evaluated is a function of the nature of the sustainability information that is the subject of the engagement. If the subject matter is a sustainability report, misstatements might be aggregated according to the nature of the matter (for example, by economic, environmental, social, and governance information) and then the effects of the misstatement(s) are evaluated individually and in the aggregate in relation to the sustainability report taken as a whole. Given the nature of different units of measurement for the different matters, the evaluation in the aggregate is performed qualitatively (see paragraph 3.63). When the sustainability information is a statement of greenhouse gas emissions, misstatements might be aggregated by type of greenhouse gas emissions. For specified indicators, misstatements are aggregated separately for each specified indicator.

3.61 When evaluating whether an omission of a needed disclosure is material, relevant considerations may include whether the sustainability information that is the subject of the engagement is misleading within the context of the engagement absent the needed disclosure (for example, whether the disclosures that are made omit any information that is needed to understand, compare, and use such sustainability information that is presented or to achieve fair presentation). Needed disclosures may be specified by the criteria or may be in addition to that specified by the criteria (for example, disclosures that the practitioner deems necessary to achieve fair presentation).

3.62 In some circumstances, materiality of misstatements may be based on the criteria (for example, it might be stated in the criteria) and the intended use for such information (for example, when the materiality of a specified indicator is established by a regulator or other filing requirement).

3.63 When evaluating the materiality of misstatements, relevant matters that might be considered include the following:

- Business purpose of the engagement
- Users of the sustainability information
- Number of misstatements
- Direction of the misstatements
- Reason for the misstatement, including whether the misstatement was intentional or unintentional
- Impact on the sustainability information, disclosures, or metrics that are significant to the company, its industry, or its regulators
- Impact on management's compensation or incentives
- Impact on trends
- Impact on commitments made by the company regarding its sustainability goals

Such considerations, including the weight given to them, are a matter of professional judgment.

3.64 To the extent the range of reasonable values exceeds materiality, the practitioner may consider whether disclosure of the uncertainty in a manner that makes it understandable, comparable, and useful to the intended report users is needed, as knowledge of the measurement uncertainty could affect the users' decisions. Disclosures of measurement uncertainty may be appropriately summarized for subtotals and totals of sustainability information rather than being reported separately for each item making up the subtotals or totals. An omission of such disclosures may be considered by the practitioner to be a material misstatement. Refer to paragraphs 4.06–.09.

3.65 Relevant considerations concerning evaluating the reporting boundary include the following:

- Whether the reporting boundary applied in preparing the sustainability information is appropriate
- Whether the reporting boundary applied in preparing the sustainability information is the same as the reporting boundary disclosed
- Whether the reporting boundary is consistent with prior periods
- Whether any changes in the reporting boundary have been clearly disclosed

Considering Subsequent Events and Subsequently Discovered Facts

Examination	*Review*
3.66E AT-C section 205 requires the practitioner to inquire whether the responsible party (and if different, the engaging party) is aware of any events subsequent to the period (or point in time) covered by the examination engagement up to the date of the practitioner's report that could have a significant effect on the subject matter or assertion and apply other appropriate procedures to obtain evidence regarding such events.[29] Paragraphs .48–.49 of AT-C section 205 include requirements of actions to take and application guidance in considering subsequent events and subsequently discovered facts in an examination engagement.	**3.66R** AT-C section 210 requires the practitioner to inquire whether the responsible party (and if different, the engaging party) is aware of any events subsequent to the period (or point in time) covered by the review engagement up to the date of the practitioner's report that could have a significant effect on the subject matter or assertion.[30] Paragraphs .31–.32 of AT-C section 210 include requirements of actions to take and application guidance in considering subsequent events and subsequently discovered facts in a review engagement.

3.67 Given the nature of sustainability information, subsequent events typically affect reported information from the perspective of considering whether disclosure of the event and its effect on the entity might be appropriate. Examples of such subsequent events include the following:

- A change in GHG emissions factors in the subsequent period
- A fatality that occurs after the end of the period that was the result of an injury sustained during the period being reported on

---

[29] Paragraph .48 of AT-C section 205.
[30] Paragraph .31 of AT-C section 210.

Performing Examination or Review Procedures

- A sale or purchase of a component after the end of the period that might have a significant effect on sustainability information reported in future periods
- A fire at a significant facility
- A change in regulatory requirements

Consistency

Examination	*Review*
Evaluating Consistency	**Considering Consistency**
3.68E With respect to the sustainability information subject to the practitioner's current year engagement, the practitioner should evaluate, as appropriate, whether the comparability of the sustainability information between periods has been materially affected by (*a*) a change in criteria, measurement method, reporting boundary, or units of measurement employed or by (*b*) adjustments to correct a material misstatement in previously issued sustainability information.	**3.68R** With respect to the sustainability information subject to the practitioner's current year engagement, the practitioner should consider, as appropriate, whether the comparability of the sustainability information between periods has been materially affected by inquiring of management whether there has been (*a*) a change in criteria, measurement method, reporting boundary, or units of measurement employed or (*b*) adjustments to correct a material misstatement in previously issued sustainability information.
3.69E The periods included in the practitioner's evaluation of consistency depend on the periods presented and the periods covered by the practitioner's opinion on the sustainability information. If an entity presents comparative sustainability information and has a change in practitioners in the current year, the evaluation of consistency includes the consistency between the year covered by the practitioner's opinion and the immediately preceding year.	**3.69R** The periods included in the practitioner's consideration of consistency depend on the periods presented and the periods covered by the practitioner's conclusion on the sustainability information. If an entity presents comparative sustainability information and has a change in practitioners in the current year, the consideration of consistency includes the consistency between the year covered by the practitioner's conclusion and the immediately preceding year.

(continued)

Examination	Review

3.70E Evaluating a change in criteria, measurement method, reporting boundary, or units of measurement employed may include determining whether
 	
   a. the disclosures related to the change are appropriate and adequate and
 	
   b. the entity has a reasonable justification for the change.
	3.70R Assessing a change in criteria, measurement method, reporting boundary, or units of measurement employed may include considering whether
	
	   a. the disclosures related to the change are appropriate and adequate and
	
	   b. the entity has a reasonable justification for the change.

3.71 A lack of comparability has the potential to mislead intended users who compare information from period to period. Factors that may affect the comparability of sustainability information between periods include a change in criteria, measurement method, reporting boundary, units of measurement employed, or adjustments to correct a material misstatement in previously issued sustainability information. The practitioner may consider whether a lack of comparability is adequately disclosed.

3.72 When an entity implements a change in criteria, measurement method, reporting boundary, or units of measurement employed to one or more prior periods that were included in previously issued sustainability information, as if that principle had always been used (commonly referred to as retrospective application), the sustainability information presented generally will be consistent. When retrospective application is used by the entity, the previous periods' sustainability information presented with the current period's sustainability information will be different from that previously reported and, accordingly, the guidance in paragraph 3.70E or 3.70R applies to such prior period sustainability information presented with the current period information.

3.73 If the entity has changed the criteria or measurement method in the current period but has not used retrospective application for any prior period information presented with the current period information, relevant considerations may include the materiality of the lack of such change to such prior period information in evaluating the effect on the practitioner's report, as discussed in paragraph 4.36.

Misstatements in Previously Issued Sustainability Information

Examination	Review
3.74E If the practitioner becomes aware of a misstatement in previously issued sustainability information, the practitioner should evaluate the effect on the current engagement. The practitioner should evaluate a correction of a misstatement in previously issued sustainability information for the purpose of determining the following: a. Whether the correction is appropriate and the effects, if any, on the measurement of the current period sustainability information subject to the practitioner's engagement b. Whether disclosures related to the correction are appropriate and adequate in the sustainability information subject to the practitioner's examination c. If the practitioner previously issued an examination or review report on such information requiring correction, whether there are any effects on the previously issued practitioner's report and related actions that the practitioner should take.	**3.74R** If the practitioner becomes aware of a misstatement in previously issued sustainability information, the practitioner should consider the effect on the current engagement. The practitioner should consider a correction of a misstatement in previously issued sustainability information for the purpose of assessing the following: a. Whether the correction appears appropriate in light of the information obtained and the potential effects, if any, on the measurement of the current period sustainability information subject to the practitioner's engagement b. Whether disclosures related to the correction appear appropriate and adequate in the sustainability information subject to the practitioner's review in light of the information obtained c. If the practitioner previously issued an examination or review report on such information requiring correction, whether there are any effects on the previously issued practitioner's report and related actions that the practitioner should take

(continued)

Examination	Review
3.75E Actions that the practitioner may take when the practitioner becomes aware of a misstatement in previously issued sustainability information include the following: • Discussing the matter with management and, when appropriate, those charged with governance • Discussing the matter with the predecessor practitioner as discussed in paragraphs 3.76–.77 • Determining whether the sustainability information needs revision and, if so, inquiring how management intends to address the matter in the sustainability information • Assessing whether steps are necessary to prevent further reliance on the misstated information • Obtaining representations from management regarding the misstatement and any correction	**3.75R** Actions that the practitioner may take when the practitioner becomes aware of a misstatement in previously issued sustainability information include the following: • Discussing the matter with management and, when appropriate, those charged with governance • Discussing the matter with the predecessor practitioner as discussed in paragraphs 3.76–.77 • Considering whether the sustainability information may need revision and, if so, inquiring how management intends to address the matter in the sustainability information • Considering whether steps are necessary to prevent further reliance on the misstated information • Obtaining representations from management regarding the misstatement and any correction

3.76 If the practitioner becomes aware of information during the examination or review that leads the practitioner to believe that the sustainability information reported on by the predecessor practitioner may require revision, the practitioner may consider it appropriate to request management to inform the predecessor practitioner of the situation and arrange for the three parties to discuss this information and attempt to resolve the matter. Relevant factors considered in determining the appropriate resolution of the matter may include the following:

- Whether the corrected information will be included for comparative purposes with the sustainability information subject to the practitioner's engagement
- The passage of time since the predecessor practitioner's report was issued (for example, if comparative information is not presented and the practitioner does not believe that it is very likely that the predecessor's report is still being relied on because of the passage of time since it was issued, the practitioner might not consider it necessary to discuss such matter with the predecessor practitioner)

3.77 The successor practitioner may communicate to the predecessor practitioner, with the permission of management, any information that the predecessor practitioner may need to consider in evaluating whether such previously reported information requires revision.

Written Representations

3.78 In addition to the written representations from the responsible party required by AT-C section 205 for an examination engagement or by AT-C section 210 for a review engagement (which includes representations regarding management's responsibility for the assertions and the subject matter, selecting the criteria and determining that the criteria are appropriate for management's purposes), the practitioner might request the responsible party to provide written representations

- Confirming management's responsibility for
    - designing, implementing and maintaining effective internal control over the subject matter;
    - determining which sustainability information is subject to the engagement (that is, specified indicators, identified section(s), or the entire sustainability report); and
    - identifying the level of assurance (that is, reasonable assurance as in an examination engagement, or limited assurance as in a review engagement) to be obtained for each of the specified indicators, identified section(s) or the entire sustainability report
- Addressing whether high measurement uncertainty exists for one or more material metrics and the nature of such measurement uncertainty

Appendix C includes illustrative management representation letters.

3.79 It is likely that the responsible party and the engaging party are the same in an examination or review engagement relating to sustainability information. If they are not the same, refer to AT-C section 205 for an examination or AT-C section 210 for a review engagement for additional requirements and considerations.

3.80 Written representations provide necessary (although not sufficient appropriate) evidence; therefore, the person(s) from whom the practitioner requests written representations is ordinarily a member of senior management or those charged with governance who has the authority to provide such representations, and is also competent to provide representations about the sustainability information, such as a chief sustainability officer.

Other Information

3.81 Sustainability information and the practitioner's examination or review report thereon often are included in documents that contain other information. In accordance with AT-C sections 205 and 210, if prior to or after the release of the practitioner's report on the sustainability information, the practitioner is willing to permit the inclusion of the report in a document that contains the sustainability information or assertion and other information, the practitioner should read that other information to identify material inconsistencies, if any, with the sustainability information, assertion or the report. AT-C sections 205 and 210 include requirements of actions to be taken if the practitioner believes that a material inconsistency or material misstatement of fact exists.[31]

3.82 If the engagement is on the entire sustainability report, other information might include a statement from the entity's chief executive officer appearing with such report. If the engagement is on specified sustainability indicators included in a sustainability report or an identified section(s), other information would encompass the rest of the document in which such specified sustainability indicators or section(s) and the practitioner's report is to be included.

Description of Criteria

3.83 AT-C sections 205 and 210 require the practitioner to evaluate whether the written description of the subject matter or assertion adequately refers to or describes the criteria.[32]

3.84 Depending on the nature of the sustainability information that is the subject of the engagement, the manner in which such information refers to or describes the criteria might vary. For example, the sustainability information might reference externally available criteria or a description of the criteria might be included in or accompany the sustainability information. As described in paragraph 1.37, an entity might use more than one set of criteria and, accordingly, might reference externally available criteria as well as include a description of other criteria in or accompanying the sustainability information.

Disclosures of Management Interpretations of the Criteria

3.85 In evaluating, based on the engagement evidence obtained, whether the presentation of the sustainability information is misleading within the context of the engagement,[33] the practitioner may consider whether management has made any material interpretations of the criteria and, if so, whether such interpretations have been adequately disclosed.

Documentation

3.86 AT-C sections 205[34] and 210[35] establish documentation requirements for examination and review engagements, respectively, together with the requirements in AT-C section 105, *Concepts Common to All Attestation Engagements*.[36] An important factor in determining the form, content, and extent of documentation of significant findings or issues is the extent of professional judgment exercised in performing the work and evaluating the results.

---

[31] Paragraphs .57 and .40 of AT-C sections 205 and 210, respectively.

[32] Paragraphs .58 and .41 of AT-C sections 205 and 210, respectively.

[33] Paragraphs .60 and .43 of AT-C sections 205 and 210, respectively.

[34] Paragraphs .87–.89 of AT-C section 205 provide additional documentation requirements specific to an examination engagement.

[35] Paragraphs .62–.64 of AT-C section 210 provide additional documentation requirements specific to a review engagement.

[36] Paragraphs .34–.41 of AT-C section 105 provide general requirements for documentation in an attestation engagement.

Documentation of the professional judgments made, when significant, serves to explain the practitioner's opinion or conclusion and to reinforce the quality of the judgment. The registry or regulatory program relevant to the attestation engagement may have additional documentation requirements for those providing assurance on the sustainability information.

Chapter 4

Reporting on an Examination or Review Engagement

Forming an Opinion or Conclusion

4.01 In forming an opinion or conclusion, AT-C sections 205, *Examination Engagements*, and 210, *Review Engagements*,[1] require the practitioner to evaluate[2]

   a. the practitioner's conclusion regarding the sufficiency and appropriateness of engagement evidence obtained; and
   b. whether uncorrected misstatements are material, individually or in the aggregate.

4.02 AT-C sections 205 and 210 require the practitioner to evaluate, based on the evidence obtained, whether the presentation of the subject matter or assertion is misleading within the context of the engagement.[3]

4.03 Aspects of sustainability information that should be considered by the practitioner in forming an opinion or conclusion on the sustainability information include the following:

   a. The overall presentation, structure, and content of the sustainability information
   b. Consistency of criteria and measurement method(s) used from the prior period
   c. The completeness of the sustainability information for the intended purpose
   d. Whether the disclosures are informative of matters that affect the use, understanding and interpretation of the sustainability information in the context of its intended purpose (see paragraphs 3.59–.65.)

4.04 Other considerations in forming the opinion or conclusion include matters such as the following:

- Whether a change in the entity's organizational boundary has occurred and whether the entity is using a consistent approach to determining its reporting boundary for preparation of the sustainability information (for example, if the organizational or reporting boundary has changed from the prior year, such as a change from reporting on the organization's domestic entities to reporting on the consolidated organization, regardless of whether comparative information is presented, whether such change is appropriately

---

[1] AT-C sections referenced in this chapter can be found in AICPA *Professional Standards*.

[2] Paragraphs .59 and .42 of AT-C sections 205, *Examination Engagements*, and 210, *Review Engagements*, respectively.

[3] Paragraphs .60 and .43 of AT-C sections 205 and 210, respectively.

disclosed and the sustainability information is appropriately labeled with the organizational boundary in the practitioner's identification of the entity).

- The adequacy of disclosures (for example, for material matters, the measurement criteria used in the current period and whether it is comparable with that used in the prior period if prior period sustainability information is presented; the source and extent of inherent uncertainties related to such information).

- Whether sustainability information is being reported publicly for the first time with comparative information and, if so, whether the process employed in the prior year in measuring and accumulating such comparative information was consistent or sufficiently rigorous to enable reporting of comparative information.

- If diagrams, graphs, or other visual representations of data are presented, whether such presentation is reflective of the actual quantitative information or possibly may be misleading.

- The consistency of narrative disclosures to tables or graphics.

- Whether errors were identified and corrected in the current period that may be indicative of errors in prior period information that is included for comparative purposes. For further guidance, see the following:

    — For the practitioner's actions when the prior period was previously reported on by the practitioner or a predecessor practitioner, regardless of whether such information is included for comparative purposes, refer to paragraphs 3.74E–.77E or 3.74R–.77R (for examination or review engagements, respectively).

    — For reporting considerations when there is a correction of a material misstatement in previously issued sustainability information, see paragraphs 4.46–.49.

4.05 AT-C sections 205 and 210 address the implications for the practitioner's opinion or conclusion when the practitioner believes that the responsible party's disclosure of matters necessary to understand, use, and compare the subject matter information (for example, measurement uncertainty) is inadequate or otherwise misleading.[4]

Measurement Uncertainty

4.06 The criteria for sustainability information may not include explicit criteria for the disclosure of measurement uncertainty. In evaluating whether the sustainability information is misleading within the context of the engagement, the practitioner should consider whether it is necessary for the sustainability information to include disclosure about measurement uncertainty, even when the criteria does not require such disclosure. The practitioner may conclude that sustainability information is misleading when it is not informative of material matters that may affect the use, understanding, and interpretation of the information, such as the extent of measurement uncertainty.

---

[4] Paragraphs .68–.81 and .51–.58 of AT-C sections 205 and 210, respectively.

4.07 When measurement uncertainty is high for sustainability information covered by the engagement, considerations may include whether and how it is communicated to report users. For example, one way of identifying and communicating such uncertainty is by disclosing the range of reasonable outcomes associated with the reported point value within which the actual value may fall.

4.08 Although the disclosures with respect to the sustainability information may be in accordance with the criteria, the criteria may not have been designed to address all reporting situations that might be encountered. In forming the opinion or conclusion, AT-C sections 205 and 210[5] require the practitioner to evaluate, based on the engagement evidence obtained, whether the presentation of the subject matter or assertion is misleading within the context of the engagement. For sustainability information that is subject to high measurement uncertainty, the practitioner may conclude that a lack of disclosure of measurement uncertainty is misleading in light of the circumstances and facts involved. To make the information reported understandable, useful, complete, and not misleading, it may be necessary for management to provide disclosures beyond those specifically required by the reporting criteria. The practitioner's evaluation of the adequacy of disclosure of measurement uncertainty increases in importance the greater the range of reasonable outcomes of the measurement is in relation to materiality.

4.09 In some cases, the practitioner may also consider it appropriate to encourage the responsible party to describe in the presentation of the sustainability information the circumstances giving rise to the high measurement uncertainty, such as by including a description of the key assumptions.

Preparing the Practitioner's Report

4.10 In accordance with AT-C sections 205 and 210, the practitioner's report should be in writing and include an identification of the sustainability information or assertion being reported on, including the point in time or period of time to which the sustainability information relates. Practitioners should not use terms such as *validation* or *verification* in their attest reports, regardless of whether the requirements of other organizations for assurance engagements use such terms because AT-C section 105, *Concepts Common to All Attestation Engagements*, requires the terms "examination" or "review" to be used to describe such engagements.

4.11 If the practitioner has been engaged to perform an examination of some specified indicators and a review of others, the practitioner should make clear in the practitioner's report which specified indicators are covered by the examination report and which are covered by the review report. Identifying the sustainability information being reported on under the examination or review engagement

    a. clarifies the level of assurance obtained by the practitioner on such information and

    b. if information that was not the subject of the practitioner's engagement is included with the subject matter, helps clarify which information is not the subject matter of either the examination or review engagement.

---

[5] Paragraphs .60 and .43 of AT-C sections 205 and 210, respectively.

4.12 To more clearly articulate what information is subject to the practitioner's examination or review engagement, the practitioner may include a paragraph disclaiming an opinion or conclusion on the information that is not subject to the engagement.

4.13 If the specified indicators are included in a sustainability report or other information accompanies the specified indicators, symbols referencing a written report that conveys the level of engagement related to each specified indicator and that is readily available may be used to identify those specified indicators that are the subject of the engagement.

4.14 If the criteria and, if applicable, significant management interpretations of the criteria are not otherwise publicly available, the criteria and description of management's interpretations should be included with the subject matter or in the practitioner's report.

Content of the Practitioner's Report

Examination Reports

4.15 Consistent with AT-C section 205, the practitioner's report on an examination of sustainability information should include the following, unless the practitioner is disclaiming an opinion, in which case items 4.15*f* and 4.15*g* should be omitted:

    a. A title that includes the word "independent".[6]

    b. An appropriate addressee as required by the circumstances of the engagement.

    c. An identification or description of the sustainability information or assertion being reported on, including the point in time or period of time to which the measurement or evaluation of the sustainability information or assertion relates.

    d. An identification of the criteria against which the subject matter was measured or evaluated. (See paragraph 4.14.)

    e. A statement that identifies

        i. the responsible party and its responsibility for the sustainability information in accordance with the criteria or for its assertion, and

        ii. the practitioner's responsibility to express an opinion on the sustainability information or assertion, based on the practitioner's examination.

    f. A statement that

        i. the practitioner's examination was conducted in accordance with attestation standards established by the American Institute of Certified Public Accountants.

        ii. those standards require that the practitioner plan and perform the examination to obtain reasonable assurance about whether

---

[6] See paragraph 4.35 regarding the inclusion of a more affirmative statement of independence in the body of the practitioner's report.

Reporting on an Examination or Review Engagement

        (1) the sustainability information is in accordance with the criteria, in all material respects (or equivalent language regarding the subject matter and criteria, see paragraph 4.16) or

        (2) the responsible party's assertion is fairly stated, in all material respects. (See paragraph 4.16.)

    iii. the practitioner believes the evidence the practitioner obtained is sufficient and appropriate to provide a reasonable basis for the practitioner's opinion.

g. A description of the nature of an examination engagement.

h. A statement that describes significant inherent limitations, if any, associated with the measurement or evaluation of the sustainability information against the criteria. (See paragraphs 4.31–.34.)

i. The practitioner's opinion about whether

    i. the sustainability information is in accordance with the criteria, in all material respects (see paragraph 4.17) or

    ii. the responsible party's assertion is fairly stated, in all material respects. (See paragraph 4.17.)

j. The manual or printed signature of the practitioner's firm.

k. The city and state where the practitioner practices.

l. The date of the report. (The report should be dated no earlier than the date on which the practitioner has obtained sufficient appropriate evidence on which to base the practitioner's opinion, including evidence that

    i. the attestation documentation has been reviewed,

    ii. if applicable, the written presentation of the sustainability information has been prepared, and

    iii. the responsible party has provided a written assertion or, in the circumstances described in paragraph .A66 of AT-C section 205, an oral assertion.)[7]

4.16 The wording of the statement of the description of planning and performing the examination discussed in paragraph 4.15*f*(ii) may depend on the nature of the sustainability information, such as described in the following examples:

- If the sustainability information is an entire sustainability report or specified indicators, the practitioner might state that those standards require that the practitioner plan and perform the examination to obtain reasonable assurance about whether the

---

[7] Paragraph .63 of AT-C section 205.

sustainability information is presented[8] in accordance with the criteria in all material respects.

- If the sustainability information is a management assertion about specified indicators being presented[9] in accordance with the criteria, the practitioner might state that those standards require that the practitioner plan and perform the examination to obtain reasonable assurance about whether management's assertion is fairly stated, in all material respects.

- When the program or registry contains specific materiality requirements that are more stringent than those of AT-C sections 205 and 210, the practitioner may include a reference to those requirements in the attest report (for example, materiality requirements under a GHG trading program or registry).

4.17 The manner in which the practitioner states the practitioner's opinion may depend on the nature of the sustainability information, such as described in the following examples:

- If the sustainability information is an entire sustainability report or specified indicators, the practitioner might state the practitioner's opinion about whether the sustainability information is [presented][10] in accordance with the criteria, in all material respects.

- If the sustainability information is a management assertion about specified indicators being in accordance with the criteria, the practitioner's opinion might state that management's assertion is fairly stated, in all material respects.

Review Reports

4.18 Consistent with AT-C section 210, the practitioner's report on a review of sustainability information should include the following:

  a. A title that includes the word "independent."[11]

  b. An appropriate addressee as required by the circumstances of the engagement.

  c. An identification or description of the sustainability information or assertion being reported on, including the point in time or period of time to which the measurement or evaluation of the sustainability information or assertion relates.

---

[8] Typically, sustainability information is in the form of a presentation and, accordingly, references might be to 'presented in accordance with' as opposed to 'in accordance with'. Whichever wording is selected, it should be used consistently between the scope paragraph and the opinion paragraph (that is, if the scope paragraph refers to 'presented in accordance with' then the opinion paragraph should use 'presented in accordance with').

[9] Typically, sustainability information is in the form of a presentation and, accordingly, management might make an assertion that the sustainability information is 'presented in accordance with' the identified criteria. If management's assertion uses 'presented', then the practitioner's report also should use 'presented'.

[10] The wording selected in the scope paragraph should be consistently used in the opinion paragraph. Accordingly, if 'presented in accordance with' is used in the scope paragraph, then the opinion paragraph should state whether the sustainability information is 'presented in accordance with' the specified criteria.

[11] See paragraph 4.35 regarding the inclusion of a more affirmative statement of independence in the body of the practitioner's report.

Reporting on an Examination or Review Engagement

d. An identification of the criteria against which the sustainability information was measured or evaluated. (See paragraph 4.14.)

e. A statement that identifies
   i. the responsible party and its responsibility for the sustainability information in accordance with the criteria or for its assertion and
   ii. the practitioner's responsibility to express a conclusion on the sustainability information or assertion, based on the practitioner's review.

f. A statement that
   i. the practitioner's review was conducted in accordance with attestation standards established by the American Institute of Certified Public Accountants.
   ii. those standards require that the practitioner plan and perform the review to obtain limited assurance about whether any material modifications should be made to
      (1) the sustainability information in order for it to be in accordance with the criteria (or equivalent language regarding the subject matter and criteria, as per paragraph 4.19) or
      (2) the responsible party's assertion in order for it to be fairly stated. (See paragraph 4.19)
   iii. a review is substantially less in scope than an examination, the objective of which is to obtain reasonable assurance about whether the sustainability information is in accordance with the criteria, in all material respects, or the responsible party's assertion is fairly stated, in all material respects, in order to express an opinion. Accordingly, the practitioner does not express such an opinion. (See paragraph 4.19.)
   iv. the practitioner believes the review provides a reasonable basis for the practitioner's conclusion.

g. A statement that describes significant inherent limitations, if any, associated with the measurement or evaluation of the sustainability information against the criteria. (See paragraphs 4.31–.34.)

h. The practitioner's conclusion about whether, based on the review, the practitioner is aware of any material modifications that should be made to
   i. the sustainability information in order for it be in accordance with the criteria (or equivalent language regarding the subject matter and criteria) or
   ii. the responsible party's assertion in order for it to be fairly stated. (See paragraph 4.20.)

i. The manual or printed signature of the practitioner's firm.

j. The city and state where the practitioner practices.

k. The date of the report. (The report should be dated no earlier than the date on which the practitioner has obtained sufficient appropriate review evidence on which to base the practitioner's conclusion, including evidence that

i. the attestation documentation has been reviewed,
ii. if applicable, the written presentation of the sustainability information has been prepared, and
iii. the responsible party has provided a written assertion or, in the circumstance described in paragraph .A49 of AT-C section 210, an oral assertion.)

4.19 The wording of the statement of the description of planning and performing the review discussed in paragraph 4.18*f*(ii) may depend on the nature of the sustainability information, such as described in the following examples:

- If the sustainability information is an entire sustainability report or specified indicators, the practitioner might state that those standards require that the practitioner plan and perform the review to obtain limited assurance about whether any material modifications should be made to the sustainability information in order for it to be presented[12] in accordance with the criteria.

- If the sustainability information is a management assertion about specified indicators being in accordance with the criteria, the practitioner might state that those standards require that the practitioner plan and perform the review to obtain limited assurance about whether any material modifications should be made to management's assertion in order for it to be fairly stated.

- When the program or registry contains specific materiality requirements that are more stringent than those of AT-C sections 205 and 210, the practitioner may include a reference to those requirements in the attest report (for example, materiality requirements under a GHG trading program or registry).

4.20 The manner in which the practitioner states the practitioner's conclusion may depend on the nature of the sustainability information, such as described in the following examples:

- If the sustainability information is an entire sustainability report or specified indicators, the practitioner might state whether the practitioner is aware of any material modifications that should be made to the sustainability information in order for it to be [presented][13] in accordance with the criteria.

- If the sustainability information is a management assertion about specified indicators being in accordance with the criteria, the practitioner's conclusion might state whether the practitioner is aware of any material modifications that should be made to management's assertion in order for it to be fairly stated.

---

[12] Typically, sustainability information is in the form of a presentation and, accordingly, references might be to 'presented in accordance with' as opposed to 'in accordance with'. Whichever wording is selected, it should be used consistently between the scope paragraph and the concluding paragraph (that is, if the scope paragraph refers to 'presented in accordance with' then the concluding paragraph should use 'presented in accordance with').

[13] The wording selected in the scope paragraph should be consistently used in the concluding paragraph. Accordingly, if 'presented in accordance with' is selected in the scope paragraph, then the concluding paragraph should refer to 'presented in accordance with'.

General Reporting Guidance

4.21 Illustrative practitioner's reports for the following are included in the appendixes noted:

- Appendix D, "Illustrative Practitioner's Examination Reports"

    — Example 1: Practitioner's Examination Report on an Entire Sustainability Report; Reporting on Subject Matter; Unmodified Opinion

    — Example 2: Practitioner's Examination Report on Specified Indicators; Reporting on the Subject Matter; Unmodified Opinion

    — Example 3: Practitioner's Examination Report on GHG Emissions Information; Reporting on the Subject Matter; Unmodified Opinion

    — Example 4: Practitioner's Examination Report on Management's Assertion About Specified Indicators; Unmodified Conclusion

    — Example 5: Practitioner's Examination Report on Management's Assertion About GHG Emissions Information; Unmodified Opinion

    — Example 6: Practitioner's Examination Report on GHG Emissions Information; Practitioner Makes Reference to the Examination Report of an Other Practitioner on a Component Entity; Reporting on the Subject Matter; Unmodified Opinion

    — Example 7: Practitioner's Examination Report on GHG Emission Reduction Information Related to a Specific Project; Reporting on the Subject Matter; Unmodified Opinion

    — Example 8: Practitioner's Examination Report on Management's Assertion About GHG Emission Reduction Information; Unmodified Opinion

    — Example 9: Practitioner's Examination Report on GHG Emissions Information; Reporting on the Subject Matter; Qualified Opinion

- Appendix E, "Illustrative Practitioner's Review Reports"

    — Example 1: Practitioner's Review Report on an Entire Sustainability Report; Reporting on the Subject Matter; Unmodified Conclusion

    — Example 2: Practitioner's Review Report on Specified Indicators; Reporting on the Subject Matter; Unmodified Conclusion

    — Example 3: Practitioner's Review Report on GHG Emissions Information; Reporting on the Subject Matter; Unmodified Conclusion

- Example 4: Practitioner's Review Report on Management's Assertion About Specified Indicators; Unmodified Conclusion
- Example 5: Practitioner's Review Report on Management's Assertion About GHG Emissions Information; Unmodified Conclusion
- Example 6: Practitioner's Review Report on GHG Emissions Information; Practitioner Makes Reference to the Review Report of an Other Practitioner on a Component of the Entity; Reporting on the Subject Matter; Unmodified Conclusion
- Example 7: Practitioner's Review Report on GHG Emission Reduction Information Related to a Specific Project; Reporting on the Subject Matter; Unmodified Conclusion
- Example 8: Practitioner's Review Report on Management's Assertion About GHG Emission Reduction Information; Unmodified Conclusion
- Example 9: Practitioner's Review Report on GHG Emissions Information; Reporting on the Subject Matter; Qualified Conclusion

• Appendix F, "Illustrative Practitioner's Report on an Examination of One or More Specified Indicators and a Review of Others, Reporting on the Subject Matter, Unmodified Opinion and Unmodified Conclusion"

4.22 The practitioner may elaborate further on management's responsibility for its assertion; for example, such as by describing management's responsibility for selecting and adhering to the criteria used or for internal control. The following such description has been illustrated in example 4 of appendix E:

> XYZ Company's management is responsible for its assertion and for the [selection *or* development of] criteria, which it has identified as an objective basis against which it assesses and reports on the selected sustainability metrics. Management's responsibility also includes the design, implementation and maintenance of internal control relevant to the preparation of selected sustainability metrics that are free from material misstatement, whether due to fraud or error.

4.23 The list of report elements in paragraphs 4.15 and 4.18 constitutes all of the required report elements for an examination and a review engagement, respectively, of sustainability information, except when one or more of the following situations is encountered:

- Reference will be made to the report of an other practitioner (see paragraphs 4.24–.30)
- There have been changes in criteria, measurement method, reporting boundary, or units of measurement (see paragraphs 4.36–.38)
- Comparative information is presented (see paragraphs 4.39–.41)
- Correction of previously issued sustainability information is made (see paragraphs 4.46–.49)

Reporting Situations Applicable to Both Examination and Review Engagements

References to the Report of an Other Practitioner

4.24 The practitioner, in his or her attest report, may refer to the report of an other practitioner under the following circumstances:

- When reporting on an attestation engagement on sustainability information and an other practitioner has reported on the sustainability information of a subsidiary or other component of the client entity

- When reporting on an attestation engagement on changes in sustainability information from one period to another (for example, when reporting on a GHG emission reduction) and an other practitioner has reported on the entity's sustainability information (for example, *GHG emissions inventory*) for the prior period

4.25 Consistent with paragraph 4.24, when the practitioner is reporting on sustainability metric reductions or progress against reduction goals, the practitioner would only be able to make reference to the report of the practitioner reporting on such metrics of a location or prior period if both practitioners are reporting at the same level of assurance on the subject matter for the same source(s) addressed by the reduction claim or goal achievement. The following examples illustrate considerations concerning referencing an other practitioner in an engagement to examine or review a reduction in total water withdrawal by source:

- If practitioner A reported on an examination of total water withdrawal by source for Plant X for which practitioner B is reporting on an examination of the reduction of total water withdrawal by source, practitioner B may divide responsibility by referring to the work of practitioner A in his or her report. However, if practitioner A reported on an examination of the company's total water withdrawal by source for its nationwide operations taken as a whole, practitioner B, who is reporting only on an examination of the reduction at Plant X, would need to perform sufficient additional procedures on the total water withdrawal by source at Plant X and would not refer to the work of practitioner A in his or her report.

- If practitioner A reported on a review of total water withdrawal by source for Plant X for which practitioner B is reporting on an examination of the reduction of total water withdrawal by source, practitioner B would need to perform sufficient additional procedures on the total water withdrawal by source at Plant X and should not refer to the work of practitioner A in his or her report.

4.26 When the practitioner decides to make reference to the work of an other practitioner in the practitioner's report on the sustainability information, the report should clearly indicate

  a. that the component was not examined or reviewed by the practitioner but was examined or reviewed, as applicable, by the other practitioner; and

b. the magnitude of the portion of the sustainability information examined or reviewed by the other practitioner.

See example 6 in appendix D and example 6 in appendix E, respectively, for illustrative examination and review reports that refer to the report of an other practitioner.

4.27 The magnitude of the portion of the sustainability information might be indicated as a percentage of the total (for example, if the sustainability information is GHG emissions, as a percentage of total GHG emissions) or as a percentage of a representative characteristic of the entity's operations (for example, if the sustainability information is a sustainability report and the other practitioner examined or reviewed the sustainability information of a subsidiary, as a percentage of total assets, net assets or total revenues).

4.28 If the practitioner decides to name an other practitioner in the practitioner's report on the sustainability information,

a. the other practitioner's express permission should be obtained, and

b. the other practitioner's report should be presented together with that of the practitioner's report on the sustainability information.

4.29 If the conclusion of the other practitioner is modified or that report includes explanatory language, the practitioner should determine the effect that this may have on the practitioner's report on the sustainability information on which the practitioner is reporting. When deemed appropriate, the practitioner should modify the practitioner's conclusion on such sustainability information or include explanatory language in the practitioner's report on the sustainability information.

4.30 If the practitioner decides to assume responsibility for work of an other practitioner, no reference should be made to the other practitioner in the practitioner's report on the sustainability information.

Significant Inherent Limitations

4.31 Identification in the practitioner's report of inherent limitations is based on the practitioner's judgment.

4.32 The following is an example of language that might be included in the practitioner's report regarding significant inherent limitations concerning the entire sustainability report:

> The preparation of [*identify the sustainability information*] requires management to establish the criteria, make determinations as to the relevancy of information to be included, and make estimates and assumptions that affect reported information. Different entities may make different but acceptable interpretations, determinations and estimates. The sustainability information includes information regarding the Company's environmental, social and governance initiatives and targets, the consideration of the estimated future impact of events that have occurred or are expected to occur, commitments, and uncertainties. Actual results in the future may differ materially from management's present assessment of this information because events and circumstances frequently do not occur as expected.

4.33 The following is an example of language that might be included in the practitioner's report when the practitioner wishes to emphasize significant inherent limitations concerning measurement uncertainty instead of or in addition to the general inherent limitations paragraph illustrated in paragraph 4.32:

> Measurement of certain amounts and sustainability metrics, some of which may be referred to as estimates, is subject to substantial inherent measurement uncertainty, including [*insert reference to measurement uncertainty disclosures in the sustainability information*]. Obtaining sufficient appropriate evidence to support our opinion [*or obtaining sufficient appropriate review evidence to support our conclusion*] does not reduce the inherent uncertainty in the amounts and metrics. The selection by management of a different but acceptable measurement method, input data, or model assumptions, or a different point value within the range of reasonable values produced by the model, could have resulted in materially different amounts or metrics being reported.

4.34 The following is an example of language that might be included in the practitioner's report regarding significant inherent limitations concerning data related to water use:

> As described in footnote(s) [*insert footnote number(s)*], measurements included in data related to water use are subject to significant inherent measurement uncertainty given the nature and methods used for determining such data. The selection by management of a different but acceptable measurement method, input data, or model assumptions, or a different point value within the range of reasonable values produced by the model, could have resulted in materially different amounts or metrics being reported.

Matters of Emphasis

4.35 The practitioner may include additional paragraphs to emphasize certain matters relating to the examination or review engagement or the subject matter that the practitioner believes are particularly relevant for intended users to understand the subject matter or the practitioner's report thereon. The following examples illustrate situations in which the practitioner might emphasize a matter about the subject matter or the attestation engagement, respectively:

- When the practitioner is engaged to report on a few sustainability indicators, the report might include an emphasis paragraph stating that the engagement was limited to those indicators selected by management and that such indicators may not necessarily reflect the overall sustainability profile of the entity.

- When a rating body or other organization requires a more explicit statement of independence be included in the body of the practitioner's report, the report might include an emphasis paragraph stating that the independence requirements of the Code of Professional Conduct issued by the American Institute of Certified Public Accountants have been complied with.

Material Change in the Criteria, Measurement Method, or Reporting Boundary

4.36 The practitioner should consider whether to include a separate paragraph in the practitioner's report when there is a material change in the criteria, measurement method, or reporting boundary. The paragraph should be included in the period of the change and in subsequent periods until the new criteria, measurement method, or reporting boundary is applied in all periods presented. If the change is accounted for by retrospective application to the sustainability information of all prior periods presented, the paragraph is needed only in the period of such change. Paragraphs 3.68E–.73 and 3.68R–.73 discuss the practitioner's consideration of situations in which the criteria have changed from prior years for examination and review engagements, respectively.

4.37 The practitioner may consider whether to include a separate paragraph when there is a change in the unit of measurement. For example, if the responsible party uses pounds in one year and tons in another, such changes might not warrant inclusion of an explanatory paragraph, provided the unit of measurement is clearly labeled. However, if the unit of measurement for customer satisfaction was changed from number of repeat purchases to the approval rating in a survey, the practitioner might include a separate paragraph describing the change, if material.

4.38 The following is an example of language that might be included for a material change in criteria, measurement method, reporting boundary, or units of measurement employed that is justified and for which there is appropriate disclosure:

> As discussed in Note X to the sustainability [report or information], in 20XX, the entity adopted a new [measurement method] for [insert description of sustainability indicator].

Comparative Information

4.39 If comparative information is presented, the practitioner's report should indicate the practitioner's responsibility for such comparative information. If such information was not subject to the practitioner's current or prior engagement, the practitioner's report should include a statement that such information was not subject to the examination or review.

4.40 The following is an example of language that might be included in the practitioner's report when comparative information is included that was not subject to the practitioner's current or prior engagement:

> The information for [insert periods presented that were not subject to a prior engagement, such as 20X1] was not subject to our [examination] [review] and, accordingly, we do not express an opinion or any form of assurance on such information.

4.41 The following is an example of language that might be included in the practitioner's report when comparative information is included that was not subject to the practitioner's current or prior engagement, but was subject to an engagement by a predecessor practitioner:

> The information for [insert periods presented that were not subject to our prior engagement, but were subject to an engagement by a predecessor practitioner, such as 20X1] was [examined] [reviewed] by another

practitioner whose report dated [*date*] expressed an unmodified [opinion][conclusion] on such information.

Modified Opinions (Examinations)

4.42 The requirements in AT-C section 205 regarding circumstances in which the practitioner should modify the opinion are applicable to sustainability information, including the requirement to express a qualified or adverse opinion directly on the subject matter, not on the assertion, even when the assertion acknowledges the misstatement.[14]

4.43 If the engagement is for specified indicators and the modified opinion relates to one or more but not all of the specified indicators, the practitioner might express separate conclusions in which an unmodified opinion is expressed on some indicators and a modified opinion on others.

Modified Conclusions (Reviews)

4.44 The requirements in AT-C section 210 regarding circumstances in which the practitioner should modify the conclusion—including the requirement to report directly on the subject matter, not on the assertion, even when the assertion acknowledges the misstatement[15]—or withdraw from the engagement[16] are applicable to sustainability information.

4.45 If the engagement is for specified indicators and the modified conclusion relates to one or more but not all of the specified indicators, the practitioner might express separate conclusions in which an unmodified conclusion is expressed on some indicators and a modified conclusion on others. However, if the effects of the matter on a specified indicator are so material that the practitioner believes that the qualification of the conclusion in the standard practitioner's report is not adequate to indicate the misstatements in the specified indicator, the practitioner actions will be based on whether the responsible party removes such specified indicator from its report:

    a. If the responsible party does not remove the specified indicator from its report, the practitioner is required under AT-C section 210 to withdraw from the engagement when withdrawal is possible under applicable law or regulation.

    b. If the specified indicator is removed from the report, the practitioner may consider whether, under the facts and circumstances, the practitioner is willing to issue a review report on the remaining specified indicators or whether to withdraw from the engagement.

Correction of a Material Misstatement in Previously Issued Sustainability Information

4.46 The practitioner should consider whether to include a separate paragraph in the practitioner's report when there are adjustments to correct a material misstatement in previously issued sustainability information on which

---

[14] Paragraph .79 of AT-C section 205.
[15] Paragraph .54 of AT-C section 210.
[16] Paragraph .55 of AT-C section 210.

the practitioner previously reported. If such a paragraph is included, it need not be repeated in subsequent periods. The paragraph may include

    a. a statement that the previously reported sustainability information has been restated for the correction of a material misstatement in the respective period, and

    b. a reference to the entity's disclosure of the correction of the material misstatement.

4.47 The following is an example of language that might be included when there has been a correction of a material misstatement in previously issued sustainability information on which the practitioner previously reported:

> As discussed in Note X to the sustainability [information or report], the 20XX sustainability [information or report] has been restated to correct a misstatement relating to [*describe indicator or matter*].

4.48 If the disclosures relating to the restatement to correct a material misstatement in previously issued sustainability information are not adequate, the practitioner should address the inadequacy of disclosure as described in paragraphs 4.02–.05.

4.49 When the previously issued sustainability information reported on by a predecessor practitioner is restated, and the predecessor practitioner has not agreed to issue a new practitioner's report on the restated sustainability information nor has the practitioner been engaged to examine or review the restated information, the practitioner should express a conclusion only on the current period and state that such restated sustainability information for the prior period has not been examined or reviewed and that the practitioner assumes no responsibility for such restated information. The illustrative language in paragraph 4.40 may be used for this purpose.

Chapter 5

Performing an Examination or Review Engagement on Greenhouse Gas Emissions Information

5.01 Greenhouse gas emissions (GHG) information is one type of sustainability information for which practitioners are engaged to perform attestation engagements. As entities often prepare separate reports on GHG information, this chapter includes specific guidance on application of the AICPA attestation standards to such separate presentations; such guidance is intended to supplement the general guidance throughout chapters 1–4 and, accordingly, should be read in conjunction with those chapters. Unless otherwise stated, the matters discussed in this chapter apply to both examination and review engagements. Although the guidance in this chapter is specific to performing an attestation engagement on a separate presentation of GHG emissions information, it can also be considered when performing an attestation engagement on a sustainability report that includes GHG emissions information.

5.02 The emphasis on attestation engagements relating to GHG emissions information in this guide is a function of the prevalence of such engagements in comparison to other sustainability information; however, it is not intended to overshadow the other topics. Over time, guidance specific to other examples of sustainability information may be added to this guide.

Introduction to GHG Emissions Information

5.03 Certain atmospheric gases (carbon dioxide, methane, nitrous oxide, and others) are called GHGs because they are believed to contribute to the retention of outgoing energy, trapping heat somewhat like the glass panels of a greenhouse. For the purposes of GHG emissions reporting by entities, GHGs include carbon dioxide (CO2) and any other gases required by the applicable criteria to be included in the schedule of GHG emissions information, such as the following:

- Methane (CH4)
- Nitrous oxide (N2O)
- Nitrogen trifluoride (NF3)
- Perfluorocarbons (PFCs)
- Hydrofluorocarbons (HFCs)
- Sulphur hexafluoride (SF6)

Gases other than carbon dioxide are often expressed in terms of carbon dioxide equivalents (CO2e).

5.04 Due to a number of global and national initiatives to reduce GHG emissions, many entities are quantifying their GHG emissions for internal management purposes, and many are also preparing a schedule of GHG emissions information, including for the following purposes:

- As part of a regulatory disclosure regime (for example, the U.S. EPA Greenhouse Gas Reporting Program; the California Global

Warming Solutions Act of 2006; and SEC Guidance Regarding Disclosure Related to Climate Change[1]).

- As part of a *GHG emissions trading program*.
- To participate in GHG emission reduction programs (see paragraphs 5.13–.16).
- To respond to shareholder resolutions calling for entities to report and have their corporate social responsibility or GHG emissions information verified by a third party.
- To inform investors and others on a voluntary basis. Voluntary disclosures may be, for example, published as a stand-alone document, included as part of a broader sustainability report or in an entity's annual report, or made to support inclusion in a public carbon registry.
- To demonstrate responsible corporate behavior.
- To satisfy requests from customers regarding information about GHG emissions within their supply chain. For example, in 2015, a new target to reduce federal government greenhouse gas emissions by 40 percent below 2008 levels by 2025 was announced. In response, in June 2016, the Department of Defense, General Services Administration, and National Aeronautics and Space Administration proposed to revise the Federal Acquisition Regulation to add an annual representation for vendors to indicate whether and, if so, where they publicly disclose GHG emissions and GHG emission reduction goals or targets.

Some entities also request verification or attestation services related to such GHG emissions information either voluntarily or in response to a requirement driven by a regulation or registry or request by other external parties, including shareholders and customers.

GHG Emissions Reporting in the United States

5.05 Voluntary reporting programs in which some U.S. entities participate include the following:

- The CDP (formerly known as the Carbon Disclosure Project), an investor-driven organization based in the United Kingdom that works with shareholders and corporations to encourage them to disclose their GHG emissions. The CDP scores entities that submit reports to the CDP on GHG emissions information based on factors such as the extent to which an entity measures its carbon emissions, the frequency and relevance of its disclosure to key corporate stakeholders, and whether the entity engages a third party to verify GHG emissions data to promote greater confidence and use of the data.
- The Climate Registry (www.theclimateregistry.org), a nonprofit collaboration among North American states, provinces, territories, and Native Sovereign Nations that sets standards to calculate, verify, and publicly report GHG emissions in a single registry.

---

[1] Code of Federal Regulations (CFR), *Commodity and Security Exchanges*, Title 17, Parts 211, 231 and 241.

Performing an Examination or Review Engagement

The Greenhouse Gas Protocol[2] is a standard that is widely used globally for the accounting and reporting of GHG emissions. Certain industries and jurisdictions require GHG emissions reporting but may not require attestation services.

Terms and Definitions Used by Registries and Regulatory Frameworks

5.06 The glossary in this guide also contains the definitions of common terms relating to GHG emissions engagements. Different registries and regulatory frameworks may use different terms and definitions for similar services, including 'validation' and 'verification,' such as described in the following:

- A validation is a service that provides assurance on the feasibility of the design of a GHG emission reduction project, usually before inception of the project; an entity typically engages an engineering or a consulting firm to provide such a service. This guide does not provide guidance on validation standards used to perform validation services.

- A verification is the objective and independent assessment of whether the reported GHG emissions information properly reflects the GHG emissions impact of the entity in conformance with pre-established GHG emissions accounting and reporting standards. A verification through an examination or review engagement performed under AICPA attestation standards may satisfy this requirement of a registry or regulator.

Various GHG registries and regulatory frameworks may not define these terms in exactly the same way; thus, the practitioner should obtain the official definitions of such terms under the registry or regulatory framework relevant to the engagement.

5.07 As indicated in paragraph 4.10, practitioners should not use terms such as validation or verification in their attest reports on GHG emissions, regardless of whether the registry or regulatory framework uses such terms, because AT-C section 105, *Concepts Common to All Attestation Engagements*,[3] requires the terms *examination* or *review* to be used to describe such engagements.

Scopes for Reporting GHG Emissions: Direct and Indirect Emissions

5.08 Reporting GHG emissions and emission reductions may encompass one or more of the following three scopes of emissions:[4]

---

[2] *The Greenhouse Gas Protocol—A Corporate Accounting and Reporting Standard* was developed by the World Resources Institute (WRI) and the World Business Council for Sustainable Development (WBCSD) to respond to the perceived need for standardized accounting and reporting of GHG emissions in connection with climate change policies.

[3] AT-C sections referenced in this chapter can be found in AICPA *Professional Standards*.

[4] *The Greenhouse Gas Protocol—A Corporate Accounting and Reporting Standard* (revised edition) (WRI/WBCSD, 2004) defines the three scopes listed in paragraph 5.08 and characterizes Scope 3 as an optional reporting category that allows for the treatment of all other indirect emissions. The definitions contained in this guide are based on those definitions.

©2017, AICPA   AAG-SUST 5.08

a. *Scope 1—Direct GHG Emissions.* Emissions from sources that are owned or controlled by the entity. The following are examples of direct GHG emissions:

   i. Stationary combustion from fuel burned in the entity's stationary equipment, such as boilers, incinerators, engines, and flares

   ii. Mobile combustion from fuel burned in the entity's transport devices, such as trucks, trains, automobiles, airplanes, and boats

   iii. Process emissions from physical or chemical processes, such as cement manufacturing, petrochemical processing, and aluminum smelting

   iv. Fugitive emissions (both intentional and unintentional releases) such as equipment leaks from joints and seals; and emissions from wastewater treatment, pits, and cooling towers

b. Scope 2—Electricity *Indirect GHG Emissions.* Emissions from the generation of purchased electricity consumed by the entity. Purchased electricity is defined as electricity that is purchased or otherwise brought into the organizational boundary of the entity. Scope 2 emissions physically occur at the facility where electricity is generated.

c. Scope 3—*Other Indirect GHG Emissions.* Emissions that are a consequence of the activities of the entity, but that occur from sources not owned or controlled by the entity. Scope 3 emissions include the following categories:[5]

   i. Purchased goods and services

   ii. Capital goods

   iii. Fuel-and energy-related activities not included in scope 1 or scope 2

   iv. Upstream transportation and distribution

   v. Waste generated in operations

   vi. Business travel

   vii. Employee commuting

   viii. Upstream leased assets

   ix. Downstream transportation and distribution

   x. Processing of sold products

   xi. Use of sold products

   xii. End-of-life treatment of sold products

   xiii. Downstream leased assets

   xiv. Franchises

   xv. Investments

---

[5] *GHG Protocol—Technical Guidance for Calculating Scope 3 Emissions* (WRI/WBCSD, 2013)

Boundaries for GHG Emissions

5.09 Determining which operations owned or controlled by the entity to include in the entity's schedule of GHG emissions information is known as "determining the entity's organizational boundary." In some cases, laws and regulations define the boundaries of the entity for reporting GHG emissions for regulatory purposes. In other cases, the applicable criteria may allow a choice between different methods for determining the entity's organizational boundary (for example, the criteria may allow a choice between an approach that aligns the entity's GHG emissions reporting with its financial statements and another approach that treats, for example, joint ventures or associates differently). Determining the entity's organizational boundary may require the analysis of complex organizational structures such as joint ventures, partnerships, and trusts and complex or unusual contractual relationships. For example, a facility may be owned by one party, operated by another, and process materials solely for another party.

5.10 Determining the entity's organizational boundary is different from what some criteria describe as determining the entity's "operational boundary." The operational boundary relates to which categories of scope 1, 2, and 3 emissions will be included in the schedule of GHG emissions information and is determined after setting the organizational boundary. Leakage may affect the choice of operational boundaries. When planning the engagement, the practitioner should obtain an understanding of the boundaries that have been set by the entity and the potential for leakage. If leakage has occurred, the entity may account for it by adjusting its *baseline* or by changing its boundaries.

5.11 Consideration of the reporting boundary is important in determining whether an attestation engagement can be performed. For example, if upstream information (for example, regarding suppliers) will be included, the practitioner will need to consider whether the practitioner is likely to be able to obtain sufficient appropriate engagement evidence for an examination or review engagement. GHG emissions information on the life cycle of a product may also provide challenges to the practitioner, given the extensive use of assumptions by management concerning the outcome of future events relating to downstream activities. This guide does not specifically address the performance of an attestation engagement on GHG emissions information for a life cycle of a product.

Base Year GHG Emissions

5.12 A meaningful and consistent comparison of GHG emissions over time requires that entities set a performance datum with which to compare their current GHG emissions. This performance datum is referred to as the base year GHG emissions.[6] Management should recalculate the base year, however, for changes in scope, boundaries, or GHG emissions accounting methodologies; subsequent acquisitions; and sales of emitting sources. If the practitioner is engaged to perform the attest service at a date considerably later than the base year, there may be differences in the quality of the data and consistency of methodology between the base year and the current year. In such circumstances, the practitioner may have difficulty obtaining sufficient evidence with respect to the base year information or the base year information may not

---

[6] *The Greenhouse Gas Protocol—A Corporate Accounting and Reporting Standard* (revised edition) (WRI/WBCSD, 2004).

be suitable for being presented in comparative form with the current year information.

GHG Emission Reduction Projects

5.13 Entities may also participate in GHG emission reduction projects to reduce the emission of GHGs, such as by setting emission limits or modifying the emission source. GHG emission reduction is measured in relation to either a base year or baseline. GHG emission reductions may be registered and traded (that is, purchased and sold by unrelated entities; for example, in an *open trading system*).

5.14 Examples of GHG emission reduction projects include, but are not limited to, the following:

- Use of renewable energy systems, such as wind, solar, and other low emission technologies, in place of higher emission technologies
- Change in processes to increase energy efficiency, such as the installation and use of more energy-efficient equipment
- Carbon sequestration: no-till farming; agricultural grass and tree plantings
- Change from more GHG-intensive fuels to less GHG-intensive fuels (for example, from coal to natural gas or nuclear power)
- Recovery and use of agricultural and landfill methane
- Improvement in the fuel efficiency of vehicle fleets
- Reduction in venting or flaring on offshore oil production platforms (installation of zero-flare systems; rapid response to unplanned events)
- Cessation of operations at noneconomical plants and transfer of production to more efficient plants
- Demand-side management projects

Attributes to Be Met by GHG Emission Reductions

5.15 Various registries and GHG emissions trading programs have specified attributes to be met by a GHG emission reduction for it to be registered or traded. Common attributes are identified and described in this paragraph; however, definitions may vary by trading program. In the context of a specific registry or GHG emissions trading program, additional requirements to be met by the GHG emission reduction may exist. Common attributes include the following:

    a. **Ownership.** In many cases, ownership is clear. Examples of such cases include efficiency upgrades at a manufacturing facility or fuel-switching at a power plant. However, for some project types, particularly those with renewable energy and demand-side management projects that *offset* or displace fossil-fuel emissions, demonstrating ownership can be challenging. Ownership of the reductions may be open to dispute because the reductions do not occur on the site of the project but, rather, on the site of a fossil-fueled facility whose power was displaced. These are known as indirect GHG emission reductions because the reductions occur at facilities other than the one where the project has been undertaken. The possibility that the direct source of GHG emissions would claim title to the

Performing an Examination or Review Engagement

same reductions claimed by the project developer or that the joint venture partners would claim title to the same reductions of their joint venture (referred to as *double-counting*) represents a risk that buyers prefer to avoid. It is possible that multiple claimants, such as the owner of the emitting source, technology vendors, and the entity installing the technology, could claim ownership of these reductions.

b. **Real.** A GHG emission reduction is real if it is a reduction in actual GHG emissions that results from a specific and identifiable action or undertaking that is not a mere change in activity level (for example, due to typical business fluctuations) and net of any leakage to a third party or jurisdiction. Leakage occurs when a GHG emission reduction project causes emissions to increase beyond the project's boundaries. Entities entering into a GHG emission reduction project typically must demonstrate that the GHG emission reduction will not cause GHG emissions to increase beyond the project's boundaries.

c. **Quantifiable or measurable.** A GHG emission reduction is quantifiable or measurable if the total amount of the reduction can be determined, and the reduction is calculated in an accurate and replicable manner.

d. **Surplus.** A GHG emission reduction is surplus if the reduction is not otherwise required of a source by current regulations or a voluntary commitment to reduce GHG emissions to a specified level.

e. **Establishment of a credible GHG emissions baseline.** Many programs measure GHG emission reductions by comparing a credible GHG emissions baseline without the project to the GHG emissions baseline with the project. A reduction quantity is not meaningful unless it is compared with a credible baseline (that is, a baseline compiled in accordance with the current protocol, using the same boundaries and scope).

f. **Unique.** Credits should be created and registered only once from a specific reduction activity and time.

Additionality

5.16 Some registries or GHG emissions trading programs may have a requirement for *additionality*. Environmental additionality requires that the GHG emission reductions achieved by the project would not have occurred in the absence of the project (the reduction must be additional to any required reductions; that is, if the entity has taken on a cap, the reduction must be additional to the cap). A credible GHG emission baseline is crucial for an entity to demonstrate additionality. Various GHG registries and regulatory frameworks may not define additionality and the terms referred to in paragraph 5.15 in exactly the same way; thus, the practitioner should obtain the official definitions of such terms under the registry or regulatory framework relevant to the engagement.

Uncertainty in the Measurement of GHG Emissions

5.17 Uncertainty in GHG emissions measurements can be due to a variety of factors. Examples of matters that may create or increase uncertainty in GHG emissions measurements include the following:

- Use of factors for which limited research or much uncertainty exists (for example, factors for CH4 and N2O from combustion processes to CO2 equivalents)
- Use of average case factors not perfectly matched to specific and varying circumstances (for example, miles per gallon, average kgCO2/MWh generated)
- Deliberate estimation to compensate for missing data (for example, facilities that are unable to provide data or missing fuel bills)
- Assumptions that simplify calculation of GHG emissions from highly complex processes
- Less accurate or less precise measurement of GHG emissions-producing activity (for example, use of standard measures of miles traveled in airplanes or rental vehicles between two points, estimation of hours per year specific equipment is used)
- Insufficient frequency of measurement to account for natural variability, such as that resulting from seasonality factors
- Limitations on the accuracy or precision of measuring instruments[7]

Objectives of an Examination of GHG Emissions Information

5.18 The practitioner's objectives for an examination of GHG emissions information typically are to obtain reasonable assurance about whether a schedule of GHG emissions information as measured or evaluated against the criteria selected by the responsible party is free from material misstatement, and express an opinion in a written report about whether

a. the entity's schedule of GHG emissions information is presented in accordance with the criteria, in all material respects, or

b. the responsible party's assertion about the schedule of GHG emissions information is fairly stated, in all material respects.

GHG Emission Reduction Information

5.19 The practitioner's objectives in an examination of GHG emission reduction information typically are to obtain reasonable assurance about whether the GHG emissions reduction information as measured or evaluated against the criteria selected by the responsible party is free from material misstatement, and express an opinion in a written report about whether

a. the entity's GHG emission reduction information related to a specific project or on an entity-wide basis is presented in accordance with the criteria, in all material respects, or

b. the responsible party's assertion about the GHG emission reduction information related to a specific project or on an entity-wide basis is fairly stated, in all material respects.

---

[7] Refer to the footnote to paragraph 1.14 regarding the use in this guide of the technical definitions for *accuracy* and *precision* that are common for engineers and scientists.

Objectives of a Review of GHG Emissions Information

5.20 The practitioner's objectives for a review of GHG emissions information typically is to obtain limited assurance about whether any material modification should be made to a schedule of GHG emissions information in order for it to be presented in accordance with the criteria selected by the responsible party, and to express a conclusion in a written report about whether the practitioner is aware of any material modifications that should be made to

    a. the entity's schedule of GHG emissions information for it to be presented in accordance with the criteria, or

    b. the responsible party's assertion about the schedule of GHG emissions information for it to be fairly stated.

GHG Emission Reduction Information

5.21 The practitioner's objective in a review of GHG emission reduction information is to obtain limited assurance about whether any material modification should be made to the GHG emission reduction information in order for it to be presented in accordance with the criteria selected by the responsible party, and to express a conclusion in a written report about whether the practitioner is aware of any material modifications that should be made to

    a. the entity's GHG emission reduction information related to a specific project or on an entity-wide basis to be presented in accordance with the criteria, or

    b. the responsible party's assertion about the GHG emission reduction information related to a specific project or on an entity-wide basis for it to be fairly stated.

Additional Considerations Regarding Preconditions for an Examination or Review of GHG Emissions Information

Assessing the Appropriateness of the Subject Matter

5.22 If the subject matter relates to information about an entity's GHG emissions, it may consist of a schedule of or an assertion on GHG emissions information, such as

- a GHG emissions inventory (an entity's emissions of GHGs for a specified period; typically, a year or a series of years, or a base year GHG emissions inventory), or
- a GHG emission reduction in connection with
    - the recording of the reduction with a registry or
    - a trade of that reduction or credit.

5.23 In assessing whether the proposed scope of the engagement on GHG emissions information is appropriate, the practitioner considers whether it covers one or more of the following:

    a. Direct GHG emissions

    b. Indirect GHG emissions associated with the generation of imported or purchased electricity, heat, or steam

    c. Other indirect GHG emissions

5.24 Some GHG emissions reporting programs may classify these GHG emissions sources differently than those noted in paragraph 5.08. The practitioner should consider the potential for double-counting of GHG emissions and reductions, especially in instances of indirect GHG emissions and shared ownership or control. If the practitioner has been engaged to report on an entity's indirect GHG emissions, especially those GHG emissions for a supplier not under the direct control of the entity, the practitioner should consider whether he or she can obtain the written representations from the responsible party believed to be necessary and obtain sufficient engagement evidence to form an opinion in an examination or a conclusion in a review engagement. The practitioner also should consider the availability or existence of data for emitting sources not under the direct control of the entity.

Assessing the Suitability of the Criteria—Additional Considerations Concerning GHG Emissions Information

5.25 Frameworks establishing criteria for a schedule or GHG emissions information usually include measurement, presentation, and disclosure considerations. Different industries, regulatory organizations, or organizations acting in a standard-setting role may have developed guidance on measurement relevant to an industry, regulated group, or GHG emissions in general. Alternatively, an entity may develop its own criteria for measurement of GHG emissions.

5.26 An entity may refine the application of measurement criteria from that included in the selected framework, perhaps using software tools for measuring GHG emissions in specific industries or using certain industrial processes, such as cement production or aluminum smelting. In these cases, the practitioner should review the entity's measurement protocol and consider whether the entity's measurement methods are appropriate.

Assessing the Ability to Obtain Evidence—Additional Considerations Concerning GHG Emission Reduction Information

5.27 As a prerequisite to performing an examination or review of GHG emission reduction information, the practitioner should assess whether the practitioner will be able to obtain sufficient engagement evidence about the entity's GHG emissions for the period in which the project took effect to provide a reasonable basis for the opinion or conclusion that is to be expressed in the practitioner's report on the GHG emission reduction information.

Other Preconditions

Independence

5.28 Certain GHG registries and regulatory frameworks set rules that prohibit professionals who provide attest services on a schedule of GHG emissions information from providing other services to the entity for a period of time. For example, a GHG framework or registry may set independence requirements that specifically prohibit a practitioner who has performed certain services for an entity from also providing a verification (that is, an examination or review) of an entity's schedule of GHG emissions information for a certain period. Such independence requirements, which may exceed those of the AICPA, or other limitations on the scope of services set by the relevant framework or registry

Performing an Examination or Review Engagement

may preclude the practitioner from performing an attestation engagement under such GHG framework or to such registry.

Professional Competence Considerations Regarding GHG Emissions Information

5.29 Knowledge about GHG emissions and competencies necessary to perform a GHG emissions engagement may include knowledge and understanding of the following:

- GHG emissions trading programs and related market mechanisms, when relevant
- Who the intended users of the entity's schedule of GHG emissions information are and how they are likely to use that information
- Applicable laws and regulations, if any, that affect how the entity should report its GHG emissions or impose a limit on the entity's GHG emissions
- GHG emissions quantification and measurement methodologies, including the associated scientific and measurement uncertainties, and alternative methodologies available
- Applicable criteria, including, for example,
   — identifying appropriate GHG emissions factors;
   — identifying those aspects of the criteria (see paragraphs 5.25–.26) that call for significant or sensitive estimates to be made or for the application of considerable judgment;
   — methods used for determining organizational boundaries (that is, the entities whose GHG emissions are to be included in the schedule of GHG emissions information); and
   — if applicable, which GHG emissions reductions are permitted to be included in the entity's schedule of GHG emissions information

5.30 In most attestation engagements on GHG emissions, the nature of the entity's operations, GHG emissions, or the GHG emissions measurement methodology in general requires specialized skill or technical knowledge in a particular field other than accounting, auditing, or attestation standards and methodologies, such as environmental engineering. The practitioner should possess adequate technical knowledge of the subject matter to understand how GHG emissions information might be misstated and to design procedures to respond to the risks of material misstatement. A practitioner may obtain adequate knowledge of the subject matter through formal or continuing education, including self-study, or through practical experience. When determining whether the practitioner has adequate technical knowledge, the practitioner should read the criteria selected by the responsible party to understand what is involved in the measurements.

5.31 Particular areas of expertise that may be relevant in such cases include the following:

- Information systems expertise, such as understanding how GHG emissions information is generated, including how data is

initiated, authorized, recorded, processed, corrected as necessary, and reported in the schedule of GHG emissions information.
- Scientific and engineering expertise, such as the following:
  — Mapping the flow of materials through a production process and the accompanying processes that create GHG emissions, including identifying the relevant points at which source data is gathered. This may be particularly important when considering whether the entity's identification of GHG emissions sources is complete.
  — Analyzing chemical and physical relationships between inputs, processes, and outputs and relationships between GHG emissions and other variables. The ability to understand and analyze these relationships will often be important when designing analytical procedures.
  — Identifying the effect of uncertainty on the measurement of GHG emissions.
  — Knowledge of the quality control policies and procedures implemented at testing laboratories, whether internal or external.
  — Experience with specific industries and related GHG emissions creation and removal processes. Creation and removal procedures for *scope 1 emissions* quantification (see paragraph 5.08) vary greatly depending on the industries and processes involved (for example, the nature of electrolytic processes in aluminum production, combustion processes in the production of electricity using fossil fuels, and chemical processes in cement production are all different).
  — The operation of physical sensors and other quantification methods and the selection of appropriate GHG emissions factors.

5.32 If the entity is a service provider whose GHG emissions are limited to the use of purchased electricity and natural gas or oil, the practitioner may be able to use published factors to convert the electricity, natural gas, or oil used to GHGs emitted to obtain evidence about how the entity calculated its GHG emissions. Under those circumstances, the practitioner may not need to use a practitioner's specialist, provided the practitioner possesses sufficient technical knowledge regarding the published factors, including an understanding of the nature of each factor and the distinctions between alternatives. If the entity has significant industrial operations with numerous sources of GHG emissions, however, it is more likely that the practitioner will need to use a practitioner's specialist.

Using the Work of an Other Practitioner for GHG Emissions Information

5.33 Examples of situations in which using the work of an other practitioner might be considered in connection with an attestation engagement on GHG emissions information include the following:

- Practitioner is engaged to examine the consolidated GHG emissions information and an other practitioner is engaged to examine such information for a subsidiary or a single facility.
- Practitioner is engaged to examine or review the GHG emission reduction information and an other practitioner examined or reviewed the GHG emissions information for a prior period. Important considerations in this situation are the level of assurance obtained by the other practitioner and the consistency of the assumptions and methods used to measure the GHG emission reduction with those used to measure the GHG emissions inventory reported on by the other practitioner.

5.34 AT-C section 105 establishes requirements for the practitioner when the practitioner expects to use the work of an other practitioner. For the practitioner to use the work of an other practitioner (for example, if an other practitioner is reporting on the GHG emissions information for a subsidiary of the entity), that practitioner also would have to perform the engagement under the attestation standards. As required under AT-C section 105, the practitioner who is engaged to report on the entity as a whole should consider whether the other practitioner has the skill and knowledge required to conduct the engagement. Other relevant information for the practitioner reporting on the entity as a whole to consider is whether the subsidiary or other entity is using the same protocol, scope of reporting, and boundaries as the parent entity. The practitioner should consider whether the other practitioner performed the examination or review considering the same level of materiality—for example, if the other practitioner performed an examination or review of the subsidiary or other entity's GHG emissions information taken as a whole.

5.35 Members of professions other than public accounting who provide verification services (see paragraph 5.06) are subject to their own professional requirements; those requirements may differ from those of the public accounting profession. Accordingly, when the practitioner is engaged to examine or review an entity's GHG emission reduction and a non-CPA has provided verification services with respect to an entity's GHG emissions inventory, the practitioner should perform procedures to obtain sufficient evidence with respect to the entity's GHG emissions inventory as part of performing the attestation engagement to report on the entity's GHG emission reduction (for example, evaluating the appropriateness of the methodology and any GHG emission factors used and whether the base year GHG emissions were adjusted if needed).

Other Engagement Acceptance Considerations Regarding GHG Emissions Information

5.36 The following are examples of additional matters that may be relevant to a practitioner's decision about whether to accept an attestation engagement regarding GHG emissions information:

- Expectations of users of the GHG emissions inventory or reduction information and the practitioner's report thereon.
- The scope of the entity's GHG emissions inventory to be covered by the examination or review engagement.
- The applicable GHG registry or voluntary or regulatory framework may set specific materiality limits. If a GHG registry or

framework sets specific materiality requirements that are more stringent than those of AT-C section 205, *Examination Engagements*, or 210, *Review Engagements*, before accepting the engagement the practitioner should consider whether it is possible to meet such requirements.

Requesting a Written Assertion on GHG Emissions Information

5.37 Examples of written assertions on GHG emissions information are as follows:

- XYZ Company asserts that its schedule of GHG emissions for the year ended December 31, 20XX, is presented in accordance with [*identify criteria selected by the responsible party*].
- XYZ Company reduced GHG emissions in connection with project ABC by 50,000 tons of CO2 equivalents for the year ended December 31, 20XX, from its GHG emissions in the prior year, based on [*identify criteria selected by the responsible party*].

Planning the Examination or Review Engagement

Obtaining an Understanding of GHG Emissions Information

5.38 In addition to the nature of procedures performed for all attestation engagements, relevant information about obtaining an understanding and other considerations when planning an examination or review of GHG emissions information typically includes the following:

- Matters applicable to GHG emissions inventories and reductions, such as the following:
    — The nature of the entity's business and whether the entity has operations and, therefore, GHG emission sources in multiple locations, and the types of GHG emissions produced
    — The business purpose or reason behind GHG emissions measurements or GHG emission reductions
    — The oversight of, and responsibility for, GHG emissions information within the entity
    — The organizational and operational boundaries used for the GHG emissions inventory
    — Whether there have been any mergers, acquisitions, divestitures, sales of emitting sources, or outsourcing of functions with significant GHG emissions that may require adjustment of the entity's base year
    — Whether all sources of emissions have been identified by the entity.
    — Sources of renewable energy (generated or purchased) that may affect calculations relating to GHG emissions

Performing an Examination or Review Engagement

- The potential for double-counting of GHG emissions and, if applicable, reductions
- When applicable, any regulatory framework(s) (for example, state- or country-specific regulations, permits, or operating licenses governing GHG emissions where the entity has operations) or any requirements relevant to a voluntary commitment to register or reduce GHG emissions
- How GHG emissions have been calculated and reported, including GHG emissions factors and their justification, global warming potentials, the mechanism by which information is managed and tracked (for example, spreadsheets or other software tools) and any assumptions on which estimates are based
- The protocols that were used for measurement of GHG emissions and whether they were used in a consistent manner throughout the entity over the period under examination or review
- Whether a third party is involved in the data capture or calculation of the GHG emission inventories, such as a bill pay provider that inputs underlying source data (for example, kWh) into the entity's data collection mechanism

- Matters applicable to GHG emission reductions only, such as the following:
  - The source of the GHG emission reduction, for instance, a switch in fuel type or change in production process (see paragraph 5.39).
  - Whether the emitting entity is required by a registry or regulatory framework to engage an outside specialist to evaluate the scientific or engineering basis for the proposed reduction project (sometimes referred to as a validation). Those rules may further specify that the outside specialist evaluating the science cannot be the same party as the verifier. When applicable, the practitioner may consider whether another reputable party has evaluated the science and found it to be acceptable and the implications of findings in the report.
  - Whether there are any ownership issues relating to the GHG emission reduction credits to be sold. For example, in the case of a landfill, the seller may own the landfill or have ownership rights over the GHG emission reduction by virtue of a contract.

Characteristics of the Collection and Reporting Processes—Consistency Considerations Regarding GHG Emissions Information

5.39 Measurement of the GHG emissions inventory requires consistent application of measurement methods. If the entity changed measurement methods during the current period, the practitioner should consider the implications on the engagement (for example, whether it is essential that the same methods be used because either comparative information is presented or a reduction is being calculated and, if so, whether the entity has restated the prior period's results using the current measurement method). (See paragraphs 1.44, 4.36, and 5.54.)

Potential Misstatements Relating to GHG Emissions Information

5.40 Examples of causes of possible misstatements of a GHG emissions inventory or GHG emissions reduction information include the following:

- Human error in calculations
- Use of incorrect GHG emissions factors or global warming potentials
- Omission from the *inventory* of GHG emissions from one or more emitting sources
- Omission from the inventory of one or more GHG emissions (for example, omission of methane emissions)
- Failure to properly account for leakage (for example, when the entity has outsourced a major function that accounted for a significant part of its GHG emissions baseline but has not adjusted its baseline to reflect such change)
- Failure to appropriately adjust the base year for events such as sales or acquisitions of GHG emitting sources
- Existence of one or more significant deficiencies in the entity's internal control over reporting of GHG emissions information
- Double counting of a GHG emission source within the entity

Considerations on Using the Work of a Practitioner's Specialist in a GHG Emissions Engagement

5.41 Examples of matters that may require the practitioner to consider using the work of a practitioner's external specialist or having a practitioner's internal specialist participate in the GHG engagement include assessing the following:

- The quality of client-provided data (for example, appropriateness and accuracy)
- The reasonableness of GHG emission factors, such as
    — whether it is necessary or appropriate to use a derived GHG emissions factor versus a published GHG emissions factor;
    — the population and selection of appropriate published GHG emissions factors; and
    — assessment of the methodology used to calculate the specific GHG emissions (see paragraphs 5.39 and 5.54)

- The work of the responsible party's specialist (for example, to assess whether the assumptions underlying the methodology are reasonable)

Illustrative Procedures

5.42 In an examination of a schedule of GHG emissions information, the practitioner chooses a combination of attestation procedures, which can include inspection, observation, confirmation, recalculation, reperformance, analytical procedures, and inquiry. In a review engagement, the types of procedures performed generally are limited to inquiries and analytical procedures (see paragraph 5.44 for further description of review procedures). Determining the attestation procedures to be performed on a particular engagement is a matter of professional judgment. Because GHG emissions reporting covers a wide range of circumstances, the nature, timing, and extent of procedures are likely to vary considerably from engagement to engagement.

5.43 Because a review engagement is substantially less in scope than an examination, the procedures the practitioner will perform in a review engagement will vary in nature and extent from those performed in an examination engagement. Paragraphs 5.44 and 5.51 describe in tabular form procedures that are relevant to examination or review engagements. Procedures that would ordinarily be performed in both an examination and a review are shown in one column across a row. Similar procedures are shown in separate columns in a row, and when a procedure is not ordinarily performed in a review engagement, the review column in that row is deliberately left blank. Although some procedures are shown only for examination engagements, they may nonetheless be appropriate in review engagements in circumstances in which procedures, in addition to inquiry and analytical procedures, are determined to be necessary by the practitioner.

5.44 The procedures listed in the following table may be performed, among others, in an examination or review of GHG emissions information, such as a GHG emissions inventory or GHG emission reduction information, to restrict attestation risk to an appropriate level for the engagement:

Examination	*Review*
a. Obtaining evidence about how GHG emissions were calculated and any underlying methodologies, emission factors, and assumptions used	a. Inquiring about how GHG emissions were calculated and any underlying methodologies, emission factors, and assumptions used

(continued)

Examination	Review
b. Evaluating the appropriateness of techniques used to calculate the GHG emissions or emission reduction, including how completeness and uncertainty are addressed in those calculations (see paragraphs 5.48–.50)	b. Considering the appropriateness of techniques used to calculate the GHG emissions or emission reduction, including how completeness and uncertainty are addressed in those calculations (see paragraphs 5.48–.50)
c. Determining whether there have been any changes in the protocol(s) used to calculate GHG emissions and, when applicable, determine whether a subsidiary uses the same protocol	c. Inquiring about whether there have been any changes in the protocol(s) used to calculate GHG emissions and, when applicable, about whether a subsidiary uses the same protocol
d. Conducting site visits as considered appropriate (see paragraphs 5.45–.46)	
e. Determining whether there have been any changes in base years, such as sales or acquisitions of operational facilities or subsidiaries	e. Inquiring about whether there have been any changes in base years, such as sales or acquisitions of operational facilities or subsidiaries
f. When applicable, obtaining information about the frequency of meter readings and calibration and maintenance of meters	f. When applicable, inquiring about the frequency of meter readings and calibration and maintenance of meters
g. Reading relevant contracts, such as for the purchase of renewable energy contracts	g. Reading relevant contracts, such as for the purchase of renewable energy contracts, as considered appropriate
h. Tracing information to supporting documents	

Performing an Examination or Review Engagement 107

Examination	Review
i. Inquiring about the existence of fraud or illegal acts or suspected fraud or illegal acts affecting the entity involving (1) management, (2) employees who have significant roles in the entity's processes and procedures relating to measurements of GHG emissions in conformity with the criteria specified previously, or (3) others when the fraud or illegal acts could have a material effect on measurements of GHG emissions in conformity with the selected criteria	
j. Inquiring about the nature of significant judgments and estimates made by management and any uncertainties regarding measurements; considering management's process for, and internal control over, developing those estimates; inquiring about key factors and assumptions underlying those estimates; and evaluating the reasonableness thereof	
k. When applicable, tracing GHG emissions factors used to recognized sources	k. When applicable, inquiring about the source of GHG emissions factors
l. Determining whether GHG emissions factors have been properly applied and whether the underlying assumptions are documented and have a reasonable basis	l. Inquiring about whether GHG emissions factors have been properly applied and whether the underlying assumptions are documented and have a reasonable basis
m. Performing recalculations	m. Performing recalculations to the extent that other review procedures are not expected to provide sufficient appropriate review evidence
n. Performing analytical procedures (for example, change in amounts from the previous year, fluctuations in amounts during the present year, and variation from an independent expectation developed by the practitioner)	
o. When applicable, comparing GHG emissions data to records of number of units sold or produced for the period	o. When applicable, performing analytical comparisons of GHG emissions data to number of units sold or produced for the period

(continued)

©2017, AICPA   AAG-SUST 5.44

Examination	Review
p. When applicable, confirming details of the transaction(s) (for example, quantity of methane sold or purchased) with the other party to the transaction	
q. Inquiring about whether there have been any changes in production levels (lower GHG emissions due to a drop in production level might not be permanent) and obtaining evidence supporting production levels	q. Inquiring about whether there have been any changes in production levels (lower GHG emissions due to a drop in production level might not be permanent)
r. Inquiring about whether there have been any communications from regulators concerning GHG emission levels or noncompliance with permits or regulatory programs	
s. Obtaining supporting evidence for any GHG emission reduction credits that are banked, purchased from, or sold to a third party (such information may be included in a public report on a GHG emissions inventory)	s. Inquiring about any GHG emission reduction credits that are banked, purchased from, or sold to a third party (such information may be included in a public report on a GHG emissions inventory)
t. Obtaining and reading environmental (or Environmental, Health and Safety [EH&S]) internal audit reports and minutes of audit committee meetings (or other relevant board committees to which the environmental or EH&S internal auditors report)	t. Inquiring about relevant information in environmental or EH&S internal audit reports and minutes of audit committee meetings (or other relevant board committees to which the environmental or EH&S internal auditors report)
u. Inquiring about whether there have been any subsequent events that would affect the subject matter or the assertion (see paragraph 5.52)	

Examination	Review
v. Requesting a legal letter when considered appropriate, for example, to address (1) noncompliance with regulatory programs [GHG emissions exceed permitted amount], (2) ownership of credits, or (3) the existence of any unasserted claims	
w. Requesting written representations from management (see paragraphs 3.78–.80 and 5.55)	

Site Visits

5.45 Site visits can provide valuable information to enable practitioners to conclude on material matters. Site visits may be needed more in an examination than a review; however, the practitioner also may make site visits to obtain certain review evidence (for example, when records are maintained at a site location, when there are significant changes at a site, or when the practitioner's initial engagement is performed). Site visits by the practitioner also may be required for reporting to a particular regulatory body or other organization.

5.46 To obtain adequate coverage of total GHG emissions, particularly in an examination, the practitioner may decide that it is appropriate to perform procedures on location at a selection of facilities. Factors that may be relevant to such a decision include the following:

- The nature of GHG emissions at different facilities.
- The number and size of facilities and their contribution to the entity's overall GHG emissions.
- Whether facilities use different processes or processes using different technologies. When this is the case, it may be appropriate to perform procedures on location at a selection of facilities using different processes or technologies.
- The methods used at different facilities to gather GHG emissions information.
- The experience of relevant staff at different facilities.
- The location of the facilities.
- Varying the selection of facilities over time.

Corroboration

5.47 In a review engagement, the practitioner ordinarily is not required to corroborate management's responses to inquiries with other evidence; however, the practitioner should consider the reasonableness and consistency of management's responses in light of the results of other review procedures and the practitioner's knowledge of the entity's business and the industry in which it operates, and the practitioner may need to perform additional procedures.

Techniques to Calculate GHG Emissions and Reductions

5.48 Reductions are calculated by comparing the amount of GHG emissions from one period to another. For entities reporting on a facility basis, this will usually be calculated annually. For entities reporting on a project basis, the period may vary depending on the nature of the project.

5.49 Measurement techniques include, but are not limited to, the use of mass balance equations, GHG emissions factors, stack tests, and direct measurement of GHG emissions, including continuous emission monitors.

5.50 For reductions calculated in comparison to a base year, adjustments are evaluated against the base year based on structural changes with the entity's organization and changes in ownership, or control of the GHG emitting source(s), or both. (Mergers, acquisitions, sales of emitting sources, outsourcing of certain functions, and entering into joint ventures would likely require adjustment of the base year.) Note that adjustments of the base year based on organic growth or decline are generally not appropriate. In circumstances in which the practitioner has previously not examined or reviewed the base year on which the reduction is being calculated (for example, in a first-year engagement), sufficient procedures should be performed on the base year to evaluate the reduction.

Procedures Specific to GHG Emission Reduction Engagements

5.51 In addition to the procedures described in paragraph 5.44, procedures that may be relevant, among others, in an examination or review engagement of GHG emission reduction information are included in the following table:

Examination	*Review*
a. Obtaining evidence of significant changes in the production process, switches from one fuel type to another, or other changes resulting in the GHG emission reduction	a. Making inquiries about whether there have been any significant changes in the production process, switches from one fuel type to another, or other changes resulting in the GHG emission reduction
b. Evaluating techniques used by the entity to calculate the GHG emission reduction (see paragraphs 5.48–.50)	b. Considering techniques used by the entity to calculate the GHG emission reduction (see paragraphs 5.48–.50)
c. Inquiring about the reason or business purpose for the reduction and considering the possible implications with respect thereto. Consider requesting from management a written representation regarding the reason for the reduction project (see paragraph 5.16 on additionality).	

Performing an Examination or Review Engagement

Examination	Review
d. Inquiring about whether there are any permits applicable to the facility and, if so, examine the permit for factors that may have a bearing on the reduction project (for example, reductions that meet other requirements cannot be transferred); requesting a management representation specific to permits	d. Inquiring about whether there are any permits applicable to the facility and, if so, about how they might bear on the reduction project (for example, reductions that meet other requirements cannot be transferred); consider requesting a management representation specific to permits
e. When applicable, reading reports prepared by the seller for purposes other than the sale of the GHG emission reduction credits (for example, a GHG emission report filed with a regulatory agency) and checking for consistency of information related to the sale	e. To the extent that other review procedures are not expected to provide sufficient appropriate review evidence, reading reports prepared by the seller for purposes other than the sale of the GHG emission reduction credits (for example, a GHG emission report filed with a regulatory agency) and checking for consistency of information related to the sale
f. Agreeing or confirming details of GHG emission reduction credits with the relevant GHG registry	f. If information is publicly available, comparing detail of GHG emission reduction credits with the relevant GHG registry

Considering Subsequent Events

5.52 AT-C sections 205 and 210 include requirements concerning subsequent events. Types of events that may represent a subsequent event in the context of an attestation engagement on GHG emissions information include the following:

- Events that would cause a change in base year GHG emissions (such as an acquisition or disposition of facilities)
- Organic changes in GHG emission levels (such as a change in number of shifts at a facility or a change in production levels)
- Destruction of the facility to which a GHG emission reduction relates
- In the case of a GHG emission reduction, unplanned or accidental release of sequestered carbon

- Investigations or regulatory actions related to GHG emissions
- Subsequent discovery of a fraudulent activity or misrepresentation relating to GHG emissions

GHG Emissions Inventory

5.53 The criteria selected are used by the entity to measure and present, and by the practitioner to evaluate, the specific subject matter of the attestation engagement. It is anticipated that appropriate disclosures will be included in the presentation, not just the quantity of GHG emissions for a period of time. The presentation may include, or be accompanied by, other information that is not subject to the practitioner's engagement, such as the discussion of the responsible party's commitment and strategy, projections, and targets related to its GHG emissions. Therefore, the form of opinion or conclusion will vary depending upon the information presented under the selected criteria on which the practitioner is engaged to report.

Evaluating or Considering Adequacy of Disclosure

5.54 The practitioner is required by AT-C sections 205 and 210 to evaluate, based on the evidence obtained, whether the presentation of the subject matter or assertion is misleading within the context of the engagement.[8] The criteria also may have specific disclosure requirements regarding consistency and completeness of sources and activities within the chosen boundary or contain principles for disclosing relevant assumptions and methodologies. Accordingly, the practitioner should consider the adequacy of disclosure of material matters. Examples of matters that may be material include the following:

- Changes in the entity's boundaries or GHG emissions calculation methodologies
- Mergers, divestitures, acquisitions, or closures
- Uncertainty in the measurement of GHG emissions (see paragraph 5.17)
- Estimation methodology used when actual data is not available

Written Representations

5.55 When the sustainability information relates to GHG emissions information, the practitioner also might request representations

- acknowledging ownership of the GHG emissions or GHG emission reductions;
- stating the absence of undisclosed or unrecorded GHG emissions sources;
- relevant to a GHG emission reduction, stating the business purpose of the GHG emission reduction project; or
- relevant to a GHG emission reduction, stating that the reduction is both real and additional to any requirements.

---

[8] Paragraphs .60 and .43 of AT-C sections 205, *Examination Engagements*, and 210, *Review Engagements*, respectively.

Other Information

5.56 If the engagement is on a GHG emissions statement, other information would likely include information submitted with the GHG emissions statement to external agencies, such as the CDP.

Documentation

5.57 The GHG registry or regulatory program relevant to the attestation engagement may have additional documentation requirements to which it may be necessary for the practitioner to adhere. For example, a GHG registry may stipulate certain documentation requirements relevant to those providing assurance on GHG emissions inventories or GHG emission reductions (sometimes referred to as verifiers).

Reporting Situations Applicable to Both Examination and Review Engagements

References to the Report of an Other Practitioner in a GHG Emission Reduction Engagement

5.58 The practitioner reporting on a GHG emission reduction would only be able to make reference to the report of the practitioner reporting on the GHG emissions inventory information if both practitioners are reporting at the same level of assurance on GHG emissions information for the same GHG emission sources addressed by the reduction project. For example, in a GHG emission reduction engagement. The following examples illustrate such considerations:

- If practitioner A reported on an examination of GHG emissions inventory for Plant X for which practitioner B is reporting on an examination of the GHG emission reduction, practitioner B may divide responsibility by referring to the work of practitioner A in his or her report. However, if practitioner A reported on an examination of the company's GHG emissions inventory for its nationwide operations taken as a whole, practitioner B, who is reporting only on an examination of the reduction project at Plant X, would need to perform sufficient additional procedures on the GHG emissions inventory at Plant X and would not refer to the work of practitioner A in his or her report.

- If practitioner A reported on a review of GHG emissions inventory for Plant X for which practitioner B is reporting on an examination of the emission reduction, practitioner B would need to perform sufficient additional procedures on the GHG emissions inventory at Plant X and should not refer to the work of practitioner A in his or her report.

Significant Inherent Limitations

5.59 The following are examples of language that might be included in the practitioner's report regarding significant inherent limitations concerning quantification of GHG emissions:

- As described in footnote(s) [*insert footnote number(s)*], greenhouse gas ("GHG") emissions quantification is subject to significant inherent measurement uncertainty because of such things as GHG emissions factors that are used in mathematical models to calculate GHG emissions, and the inability of these models, due to incomplete scientific knowledge and other factors, to accurately measure under all circumstances the relationship between various inputs and the resultant GHG emissions. Environmental and energy use data used in GHG emissions calculations are subject to inherent limitations, given the nature and methods used for measuring such data. The selection by management of a different but acceptable measurement method, input data, or model assumptions, or a different point value within the range of reasonable values produced by the model, could have resulted in materially different amounts or metrics being reported.
- As described in footnote X, environmental and energy use data are subject to measurement uncertainty resulting from limitations inherent in the nature and methods used for determining such data. The selection by management of a different but acceptable measurement method, input data or model assumptions, or a different point value within the range of reasonable values produced by the model, could have resulted in materially different amounts or metrics being reported.

Matters of Emphasis

5.60 When the practitioner is engaged to report on GHG emissions of one or more particular locations or subsidiaries or on reductions related to one or more specific projects, the practitioner might include a paragraph in the practitioner's report stating that the practitioner was not engaged to examine or review the entity-wide GHG emissions or reductions and, accordingly, the practitioner is not expressing any form of opinion or conclusion on such entity-wide information.

Comparative Information

5.61 If the sustainability information is GHG emissions information and the responsible party does not appropriately restate the base year and prior period inventory comparative information for a material change, the practitioner should include an explanatory paragraph in the practitioner's report describing the lack of consistency and should express a qualified or adverse opinion in an examination report or a modified conclusion in a review report due to a departure from the criteria.

Appendix A

Illustrations of Measurements and Measurement Uncertainty

This appendix is nonauthoritative and is included for informational purposes only.

The following illustrations of measurements and measurement uncertainty are provided for purposes of aiding practitioners in identifying and considering sources of measurement uncertainty in sustainability metrics.

1) **Measurement of CO2 emissions from air travel by company personnel**

   The company measures CO2 emissions from air travel based on information provided by its travel agent and the commercial airlines. Its travel agent accumulates data from the airlines on employee travel booked by the travel agent, which is recorded in its information system and periodically supplied to the company. Some travel by executives is for both personal and business reasons. Whether the information is reported by the travel agent as business CO2 emissions depends on the coding by the executive (or executive assistant). (The CO2 emissions reported by the airlines to the travel agent and the accumulation and reporting by the travel agent are sources of *nonstatistically estimated measurement uncertainty*.) On occasion, an executive may book a business trip directly with an airline or through another online travel agent such that the CO2 emissions of that trip are not captured by the company's travel agent (this is another source of nonstatistically estimated measurement uncertainty). The information gathered by the company's travel agent from the airlines is standard CO2 information based on type of aircraft scheduled and the typical distance traveled.

   Measurement uncertainty for the information provided by the airlines arises from measurement of emissions from a sample of engines and aircraft combinations. The range of reasonable outcomes (measurement uncertainty) depends, in part, on the sample size and the variability of emissions observed in the sample. The extent of this source of measurement uncertainty may be estimated by the airline through statistical means based on the results of multiple test measurements and supplied to the travel agent and others. Measurement uncertainty also arises from the fact that the aircraft used may not be of the type promised on the ticket; the actual aircraft used may have a different efficiency than the standard aircraft (for example, due to the type of engines, state of maintenance); the load (weight) of the particular flight may be different than the standard; and the flight path and headwinds may be different than the standard. (The use of a standard flight between two destinations for a given aircraft type is a source of measurement uncertainty that may need to be estimated through nonstatistical means). The aircraft also emits methane, a greenhouse gas, that for purposes of the greenhouse gas emission statement is converted to an equivalent mass of CO2 using a conversion factor that is updated from time to time (the standard conversion factor, and the determination of the conversion factor used by the airlines based on samples, are sources of measurement uncertainty; the latter is a source of *statistically estimated measurement uncertainty*). The equivalent CO2 is included in the information reported by the airline for each flight. The emission of methane during any given flight is subject to the same variables that affect CO2 emissions described above.

2) **Measurement of water use**

The company uses water for many purposes from many different sources. It has several processes in place to capture each use of water and measure the company's consumption. However, due to the number of facilities and sources of water used, these measurements vary in completeness, consistency, and accuracy. For example, some water is pumped directly from natural sources (for example, rivers, lakes, reservoirs and collected runoff) and the measurement of such, when it occurs, may not be accurate due to the age and reliability of meters employed and leakage. (Even though periodic measurement with more precise meters is used on a sample basis, this process is subject to random sources of inaccuracy and imprecision, which results in measurement uncertainty.) Some water is purchased from water suppliers and metered by such water suppliers. Their metering is subject to measurement uncertainty due to the inherent accuracy and precision of their meters. (The accuracy of the meters is tested and calibrated periodically, such that the sampling used for the testing and the calibration processes are sources of measurement uncertainty that may be estimated through statistical means.) Also, the measurements and billing statements supplied by the water suppliers are not usually exactly consistent with the company's reporting period, so allocations must be made to days that are within the company's reporting period based on daily average consumption during the billing period, even though that may not be exact usage for the reporting period (another source of measurement uncertainty).

Further, the company's reporting boundary for water consumption includes that of several hundred business affiliates, some of whom report more consistently and timely than others. As a result, the accumulated consumption from those affiliates is typically somewhat incomplete despite the company's efforts to follow up. Therefore, the company has in place a process to estimate the missing water consumption based on the past history of the particular affiliate and time period of missing data (another source of measurement uncertainty). For some new affiliates, water consumption information is not available for a period of time until the reporting process can be established. That missing information is considered to be not significant (but is another source of measurement uncertainty).

Appendix B

Characteristics of Sustainability Information and Illustrative Examination and Review Procedures

This appendix is nonauthoritative and is included for informational purposes only.

The following table illustrates the manner in which the characteristics of sustainability information described in paragraph 2.05 of this guide apply to sustainability information, together with illustrative procedures that might be performed, and it differentiates the nature of the work between an examination and a review engagement on an entire sustainability report. Because materiality considerations might change from the report as a whole to each specified indicator, if the practitioner is engaged to examine or review specified indicators, the extent of procedures for such an opinion or conclusion may be more extensive for each specified indicator than they would be for an examination or review engagement on an entire sustainability report. The type of the procedures is also affected by the criteria that the information is to be measured or evaluated against.

Note: It is assumed in the description of procedures below that the practitioner is also the financial statement auditor and, accordingly, is able to use the knowledge obtained from the financial statement audit and, if applicable, other services provided to the entity. (See paragraph 2.07 for relevant matters that might be considered when the practitioner is not the financial statement auditor or independent public accountant and for relevant considerations with regard to when the practitioner is engaged to perform the examination or review engagement with respect to specified indicators).

Characteristic of Information		Examples	Types of Procedures	
			Examination	Review
Quantified measurements	Amounts	• Number of countries in which the entity operates	• Evaluate listing for consistency with knowledge of entity • Inquiries of management • Comparison of the listing of countries with other records (for example, payroll records, tax filings) • Comparison to information shared publicly (for example, on the entity's website, in press releases)	• Evaluate listing for consistency with knowledge of entity • Inquiries of management

(continued)

Characteristic of Information	Examples	Types of Procedures	
		Examination	Review
	• Number of employees	• Analytical review of analysis of employees by location • Reconciliation to payroll records • Tests of reconciliation • Comparison to reports submitted to governmental entities, including tax reporting	• Analytical review of analysis of employees by location • Reconciliation of significant or higher risk location(s) to payroll records
	• Revenues	• Comparison to audited F/S	• Comparison to audited F/S
	• Economic value distributed[1]	• Comparison of components to audited F/S • Analytical procedures • Recalculations	• Comparison of components to audited F/S • Analytical procedures • Recalculations (extent less than for an examination)
	• Scope 2 emissions	• Inquiries of how the measurements, including estimates, are derived • Obtaining an understanding of the measurement process and model(s) used • Analytical procedures • Tests of data and evaluations of key assumptions and factors used in the measurement	• Inquiries of how the measurements, including estimates, are derived • Analytical procedures • Recalculations (extent less than for an examination)

[1] *Economic value distributed* is defined by the Global Reporting Initiative's G4 Sustainability Reporting Guidelines as operating costs, employee wages and benefits, payments to providers of capital, payments to government (by country), and community investments.

Characteristics of Sustainability Information and Illustrative Procedures

Characteristic of Information		Examples	Types of Procedures	
			Examination	*Review*
	Percentages	• % of employees covered by collective bargaining agreements	• Inquiries as to how the numerator and denominator are derived • Analytical procedures on the numerator and denominator, or on the percentage(s) • Testing of the accuracy of population comprising the numerator and denominator • Recalculations	• Inquiries as to how the numerator and denominator are derived • Analytical procedures on the numerator and denominator, or on the percentage(s) • Recalculations (extent less than for an examination)
	Targets	• GHG emission reduction goals • Planned proportion of women and minorities on the board of directors	• Inquiries as to basis for targets • Comparison with reported achievements for current and prior years • Comparison to budgets, plans, and other strategy documents • Review of board meeting minutes	• Inquiries as to basis for targets • Comparison with reported achievements for current and prior years (extent less than for an examination)
Factual narrative		• Description of governance	• Comparison with information reported on the entity's website • Comparison with other publicly available documents (for example, public entity filings) • Comparison with board and board committee meeting minutes, charters, and bylaws • Reading analyst and proxy research firm reports evaluating governance • Inquiries of management	• Comparison with information reported on the entity's website • Comparison with other publicly available documents (for example, public entity filings) • Inquiries of management

(continued)

| | | | Types of Procedures ||
Characteristic of Information		Examples	Examination	Review
		• Composition of board and committees	• Comparison with information reported on the entity's website, proxy statements (public companies), and other documentation • Inquiries of management as to whether there have been any recent changes	• Comparison with information reported on the entity's website or proxy statements • Inquiries of management as to whether there have been any recent changes
		• Description of key impacts on sustainability	• Inquiries as to the basis for such assertions • Comparisons with documents used by management as a basis for the assertion • Obtaining an understanding of the process and model(s) used by management to prepare the assertion • Tests of data and evaluations of key assumptions used in preparing the assertion	• Inquiries as to the basis for such assertions • Comparisons with documents used by management as a basis for the assertion (extent less than for an examination)
Soft narrative		• Statement of vision and strategy	• Inquiries of senior management • Comparison with internal documents • Comparison with the practitioner's knowledge of the entity	• Inquiries of senior management • Comparison with the practitioner's knowledge of the entity

Characteristics of Sustainability Information and Illustrative Procedures

Characteristic of Information		Examples	Types of Procedures	
			Examination	Review
		• Description of risks and opportunities	• Inquiries of key financial and operational management; consideration with existing business knowledge • Inspection of internal documents • Comparison to risk factors disclosed in public filings • Comparison to risk factors disclosed to industry information	• Inquiries of key financial and operational management; consideration with existing business knowledge • Inspection of internal documents (extent less than for an examination)
		• Description of remuneration policies	• Inquiries of senior management • Inquiries of the compensation committee or board of directors • Comparison with other documentation (for example, disclosures on remuneration policies included in public filings) • Comparison with payroll and other records	• Inquiries of senior management • Comparison with other documentation
		• Description of processes	• Inquiries of different individuals • Comparison with written descriptions provided to employees, posted to internal or external websites, or otherwise made available to others • Walkthroughs (reperformance) of the processes	• Inquiries of different individuals • Inspection of written materials

(continued)

Characteristic of Information		Examples	Types of Procedures	
			Examination	Review
Diagrams or graphs		• Charts, graphs and infographics	• Comparisons of amounts with supporting documentation • Testing of information underlying the chart • Consideration as to whether the form and scale of the diagram, graph, or infographic portrays the information in a reasonable and not misleading manner, without bias	• Comparisons of amounts with supporting documentation (extent less than for an examination) • Consideration as to whether the form and scale of the diagram, graph, or infographic portrays the information in a reasonable and not misleading manner, without bias

Appendix C

Illustrative Representation Letters and Additional Representations

This appendix is nonauthoritative and is included for informational purposes only.

The following representation letters illustrate the requirements for written representations in AT-C sections 205, *Examination Engagements*, and 210, *Review Engagements* (AICPA, *Professional Standards*), and the additional representations specific to sustainability information in paragraph 3.78 of this guide.

> Example 1: Illustrative representation letter when reporting on the subject matter
>
> Example 2: IIlustrative representation letter when reporting on an assertion(s)
>
> Example 3: Additional representations for GHG emission reductions

Example 1

1 Illustrative Representation Letter When Reporting on the Subject Matter

[*Date*]

[*Name of CPA Firm*]

We are providing this letter in connection with your [*examination / review*] of [*describe subject matter*[1] *and criteria, or for specified indicators, a reference to a table within the representation letter identifying the specified indicators and criteria*] (the "subject matter").

We confirm that we are responsible for the subject matter and designing, implementing, and maintaining effective internal control over the sustainability information. We also confirm that we are responsible for determining which sustainability information is subject to your [*examination / review*] and identifying the level of assurance to be obtained for [each of the specified indicators/the identified section(s)/the entire sustainability report]. We further confirm that we are responsible for the selection of [*identify criteria*] as the criteria against which you are evaluating the subject matter. Further, we confirm that we are responsible for determining that [*identify criteria*] represent appropriate criteria for our purposes and for making and disclosing all needed interpretations of such criteria.

We confirm, to the best of our knowledge and belief, the following representations made to you during your [*examination / review*]:

---

[1] Examples of a description of the subject matter include the following:
- XYZ Company's sustainability report for the year ended December 31, 20XX presented in accordance with [*identify criteria*]
- The schedule of greenhouse gas (GHG) emissions of XYZ Company for the year ended December 31, 20XX presented in accordance with [*identify criteria used; for example*, The Greenhouse Gas Protocol—A Corporate Accounting and Reporting Standard (revised edition) *and the* Corporate Value Chain [Scope 3] Accounting and Reporting Standard, *published by the World Business Council for Sustainable Development (WBCSD) and the World Resource Institute (WRI)*].

1. [State that the subject matter has been prepared in accordance with the stated criteria; for example, XYZ Company's sustainability report for the year ended December 31, 20XX is presented[2] in accordance with [identify the criteria].]

2. All relevant matters are reflected in the measurement or evaluation of the subject matter. Significant assumptions used in making material estimates are reasonable.[3]

3. All known matters contradicting the subject matter, and any communications from regulatory agencies or [identify organizations; for example, organizations to which the company reports GHG emissions] affecting the subject matter have been disclosed to you, including communications received subsequent to the period being reported on and through the date of this letter.

4. [For GHG emissions: We have disclosed to you all significant emission sources. There are no material emissions that have not been recorded in the greenhouse gas (GHG) emission records underlying our assertion(s) referred to above. GHG emissions have been reported for the entities where the Company has operational control.]

5. We have disclosed to you our knowledge of any actual, suspected, or alleged fraud or noncompliance with laws or regulations affecting the subject matter, including (a) fraud involving management or employees who have significant roles in the Company's processes and procedures relating to measurements of [describe; for example, emissions] in conformity with the criteria specified above, and (b) fraud involving others that could have a material effect on measurements of [describe; for example, emissions] in conformity with the selected criteria.

6. We have disclosed to you all deficiencies in the design or operation of the Company's internal control over the subject matter of which we are aware.

7. We have provided you with all relevant information and access to records relevant to your [examination / review] of the subject matter.

8. We have responded fully to all inquiries made by you during the engagement.

9. We have disclosed to you events that occurred subsequent to the period being reported on and through the date of this letter that would have a material effect on the subject matter or assertion(s).

10. [Add additional representations as deemed appropriate.]

---

[2] Typically, sustainability information is in the form of a presentation and, accordingly, might be described as being "presented in accordance with" the identified criteria. Refer to paragraph 4.16 for an examination engagement and paragraph 4.19 for a review engagement regarding the use of 'presented' and implications for the practitioner's report. If the practitioner's report will be using 'presented in accordance with,' similar terminology would be included in the management representation letter. This applies to all subsequent references in this appendix to "presented in accordance with."

[3] The practitioner may wish to obtain additional representations regarding measurement uncertainty, such as the following:

> We have not identified high measurement uncertainty (measurement uncertainty in excess of [specify amount]), other than as disclosed in [identify presentation of sustainability information].

[If misstatements have been identified that were not corrected: We believe the effects of uncorrected misstatements [listed in the accompanying summary of uncorrected misstatements] are immaterial individually and in the aggregate, to the subject matter.]

[Name of responsible officer and title]

[Name(s) of other appropriate officer(s) or management representative(s) and title(s)[4]]

Example 2

Illustrative Representation Letter When Reporting on an Assertion/(s)

[Date]

[Name of CPA Firm]

We are providing this letter in connection with your [examination/review] of our [describe the assertion(s)[5] and criteria] (the "assertion").

We confirm that we are responsible for the assertion and designing, implementing, and maintaining effective internal control over the sustainability information. We also confirm that we are responsible for determining which sustainability information is subject to your [examination/review] and identifying the level of assurance to be obtained for [each of the specified indicators/the identified section(s)/the entire sustainability report]. We further confirm that we are responsible for the selection of [identify criteria] as the criteria against which you are evaluating our assertion(s). Further, we confirm that we are responsible for determining that [identify criteria] represent appropriate criteria for our purposes and for making and disclosing all needed interpretations of such criteria.

We confirm, to the best of our knowledge and belief, the following representations made to you during your [examination/review]:

1. [Include the assertion(s) about the subject matter or, if the assertion is stated in the opening paragraph, Our assertion(s) identified above is(are) fairly stated.]
2. All relevant matters are reflected in the measurement or evaluation of the subject matter underlying our assertion(s). Significant assumptions used in making material estimates are reasonable.[6]

---

[4] Officers and other management representatives may vary, depending on the circumstances.

[5] Examples of an assertion include the following:

- Our assertion that XYZ Company's sustainability report for the year ended December 31, 20XX is presented in accordance with [identify criteria].
- The schedule of greenhouse gas (GHG) emissions of XYZ Company for the year ended December 31, 20XX presented in accordance with [identify criteria used; for example, The Greenhouse Gas Protocol—A Corporate Accounting and Reporting Standard (revised edition) and the Corporate Value Chain [Scope 3] Accounting and Reporting Standard, published by the World Business Council for Sustainable Development (WBCSD) and the World Resource Institute (WRI)].

[6] The practitioner may wish to obtain additional representations regarding measurement uncertainty, such as the following:

We have not identified high measurement uncertainty (measurement uncertainty in excess of [specify amount]), other than as disclosed in [identify presentation of sustainability information].

3. All known matters contradicting our assertion(s), and any communications from regulatory agencies or [*identify organizations; for example, organizations to which the company reports GHG emissions*] affecting the subject matter or our assertion(s) on such subject matter have been disclosed to you, including communications received subsequent to the period being reported on and through the date of this letter.

4. [*For GHG emissions:* We have disclosed to you all significant emission sources. There are no material emissions that have not been recorded in the greenhouse gas (GHG) emission records underlying our assertion(s) referred to above. GHG emissions have been reported for the entities where the Company has operational control.]

5. We have disclosed to you our knowledge of any actual, suspected, or alleged fraud or noncompliance with laws or regulations affecting [*identify subject matter of the assertion(s)*] including (*a*) fraud involving management or employees who have significant roles in the Company's processes and procedures relating to measurements of [*describe; for example, emissions*] in conformity with the criteria specified above, and (*b*) fraud involving others that could have a material effect on measurements of [*describe; for example, emissions*] in accordance with the selected criteria.

6. We have disclosed to you all deficiencies in the design or operation of the Company's internal control over its [*describe subject matter underlying the assertion; for example, GHG emissions inventory*] of which we are aware.

7. We have provided you with all relevant information and access to records concerning the underlying subject matter relevant to your [*examination/review*] of the assertion(s).

8. We have responded fully to all inquiries made by you during the engagement.

9. We have disclosed to you events that occurred subsequent to the period being reported on and through the date of this letter that would have a material effect on the subject matter or assertion(s)

10. [*Add additional representations as deemed appropriate.*]

[*If misstatements have been identified that were not corrected:* We believe the effects of uncorrected misstatements [listed in the accompanying summary of uncorrected misstatements] are immaterial individually and in the aggregate, to the subject matter.]

[*Name of responsible officer and title*]

[*Name(s) of other appropriate officer(s) or management representative(s) and title(s)*[7]]

---

[7] Officers and other management representatives may vary depending on the circumstances.

Example 3

Additional Representations for GHG Emission Reductions

The following illustrates an example of a written assertion and additional representations that should be obtained in connection with GHG emission reductions:

Example assertion in connection with an emission reduction:

> XYZ Company reduced GHG emissions in connection with project ABC by 50,000 tons of CO2 equivalents for the year ended December 31, 20XX, based on [*identify criteria selected by the responsible party*].
>
> *Additional representations:*
>
> The GHG emission reduction project was undertaken for the purpose of [*describe business purpose*]. The GHG emission reductions were achieved as a direct result of the project and not as a result of any changes in activity level. The GHG emission reductions related to the project are both real and additional to any requirements. Further, we have satisfactory title to all GHG emission reduction credits related to the project, and there are no liens or encumbrances on such GHG emission reduction credits, nor have any GHG emission reduction credits been pledged as collateral.

Appendix D

Illustrative Practitioner's Examination Reports

This appendix is nonauthoritative and is included for informational purposes only.

The illustrative examination reports included in this appendix are provided for a few of the common reporting situations that a practitioner might encounter with respect to sustainability information but are not intended to be a complete list. These reports are intended for general use situations. See paragraphs .64–.66 of AT-C section 205, *Examination Engagements* (AICPA, *Professional Standards*), for requirements and guidance on restricting the use of an examination report.

Example 1: Practitioner's Examination Report on an Entire Sustainability Report; Reporting on Subject Matter; Unmodified Opinion

Example 2: Practitioner's Examination Report on Specified Indicators; Reporting on the Subject Matter; Unmodified Opinion

Example 3: Practitioner's Examination Report on GHG Emissions Information; Reporting on the Subject Matter; Unmodified Opinion

Example 4: Practitioner's Examination Report on Management's Assertion About Specified Indicators; Unmodified Conclusion

Example 5: Practitioner's Examination Report on Management's Assertion About GHG Emissions Information; Unmodified Opinion

Example 6: Practitioner's Examination Report on GHG Emissions Information; Practitioner Makes Reference to the Examination Report of an Other Practitioner on a Component Entity; Reporting on the Subject Matter; Unmodified Opinion

Example 7: Practitioner's Examination Report on GHG Emission Reduction Information Related to a Specific Project; Reporting on the Subject Matter; Unmodified Opinion

Example 8: Practitioner's Examination Report on Management's Assertion About GHG Emission Reduction Information; Unmodified Opinion

Example 9: Practitioner's Examination Report on GHG Emissions Information; Reporting on the Subject Matter; Qualified Opinion

Example 1: Practitioner's Examination Report on an Entire Sustainability Report; Reporting on Subject Matter; Unmodified Opinion

Independent Accountant's Report

[*Appropriate Addressee*]

We have examined [*identify the subject matter, for example, XYZ Company's sustainability report for the year ended December 31, 20XX*]. XYZ Company's management is responsible for preparing and presenting [*identify the subject matter, for example, XYZ Company's sustainability report*] in accordance with [*identify the criteria, for example, the criteria specified on page XX of the accompanying sustainability report*]. Our responsibility is to express an opinion on [*identify the* subject matter, for example, XYZ Company's sustainability report] based on our examination.

Our examination was conducted in accordance with attestation standards established by the American Institute of Certified Public Accountants. Those standards require that we plan and perform the examination to obtain reasonable assurance about whether [identify the subject matter, for example, the sustainability report] is presented in accordance with the criteria, in all material respects. An examination involves performing procedures to obtain evidence about [identify the subject matter, for example, the sustainability report]. The nature, timing, and extent of the procedures selected depend on our judgment, including an assessment of the risks of material misstatement of [identify the subject matter, for example, the sustainability report], whether due to fraud or error. We believe that the evidence we obtained is sufficient and appropriate to provide a reasonable basis for our opinion.

[Include a description of significant inherent limitations, if any, associated with the measurement or evaluation of the subject matter against the criteria, such as measurement uncertainty. See paragraphs 4.32–.34 and 5.59 for illustrative language.]

[Additional paragraph(s) may be added to emphasize certain matters relating to the examination engagement or the subject matter. See paragraph 4.35.]

In our opinion, [identify the subject matter, for example, XYZ Company's sustainability report] is presented in accordance with [identify the criteria, for example, the criteria specified within the report] in all material respects.

[Practitioner's signature]
[Practitioner's city and state]
[Date of practitioner's report]

Example 2: Practitioner's Examination Report on Specified Indicators; Reporting on the Subject Matter; Unmodified Opinion

Illustrative opinion paragraphs are also illustrated below for when the subject matter is a specified section of a sustainability report.

Independent Accountant's Report

[Appropriate Addressee]

We have examined [identify the subject matter, for example, the following specified indicators included in XYZ Company's sustainability report for the year ended December 31, 20XX].

- [Indicator 1]
- [Indicator 2]

XYZ Company's management is responsible for [identify the subject matter, for example, preparing and presenting the above specified indicators] in accordance with [identify the criteria, for example, the criteria specified on page XX of the accompanying sustainability report]. Our responsibility is to express an opinion on [identify the subject matter, for example, the specified indicators] based on our examination.

Our examination was conducted in accordance with attestation standards established by the American Institute of Certified Public Accountants. Those standards require that we plan and perform the examination to obtain reasonable assurance about whether [*identify the subject matter, for example, the specified indicators*] are/is presented in accordance with the criteria, in all material respects. An examination involves performing procedures to obtain evidence about [*identify the subject matter, for example, the specified indicators*]. The nature, timing, and extent of the procedures selected depend on our judgment, including an assessment of the risks of material misstatement of [*identify the subject matter, for example, the specified indicators*], whether due to fraud or error. We believe that the evidence we obtained is sufficient and appropriate to provide a reasonable basis for our opinion.

[*Include a description of significant inherent limitations, if any, associated with the measurement or evaluation of the subject matter against the criteria, such as measurement uncertainty. See paragraphs 4.32–.34 and 5.59 for illustrative language.*]

[*Additional paragraph(s) may be added to emphasize certain matters relating to the examination engagement or the subject matter. See paragraph 4.35.*]

In our opinion, [*identify the subject matter, for example, the specified indicators referred to above*] are/is presented in accordance with [*identify the criteria, for example, the criteria specified within the report*] in all material respects.

[*Practitioner's signature*]

[*Practitioner's city and state*]

[*Date of practitioner's report*]

Opinion paragraph covering a specified section of a sustainability report:

In our opinion, [*identify the subject matter, for example, specify the applicable section*] of [*identify the report that the subject matter is included in, for example, the 20XX sustainability report of XYZ Company*] is presented in accordance with [*identify the criteria*], in all material respects.

Depending on the nature of, and information included in, the specified section, the following might be an appropriate alternative:

In our opinion, the information provided in [*specify the subject matter section*] in the accompanying [*identify the report that the subject matter is included in, for example, the 20XX sustainability report of XYZ Company*] is presented in accordance with [*identify the criteria*], in all material respects.

Example 3: Practitioner's Examination Report on GHG Emissions Information; Reporting on the Subject Matter; Unmodified Opinion

Independent Accountant's Report

[*Appropriate Addressee*]

We have examined the accompanying schedule of greenhouse gas emissions of XYZ Company for [*identify the period, for example, the year ended December 31, 20XX]*. XYZ Company's management is responsible for preparing and presenting the schedule of greenhouse gas emissions in accordance with *[identify the criteria]*. Our responsibility is to express an opinion on the schedule of greenhouse gas emissions based on our examination.

Our examination was conducted in accordance with attestation standards established by the American Institute of Certified Public Accountants. Those standards require that we plan and perform the examination to obtain reasonable assurance about whether the schedule of greenhouse gas emissions is presented in accordance with the criteria, in all material respects. An examination involves performing procedures to obtain evidence about *[identify the subject matter; for example, the schedule of greenhouse gas emissions]*. The nature, timing, and extent of the procedures selected depend on our judgment, including an assessment of the risks of material misstatement of the schedule of greenhouse gas emissions, whether due to fraud or error. We believe that the evidence we obtained is sufficient and appropriate to provide a reasonable basis for our opinion.

[Include a description of significant inherent limitations, if any, associated with the measurement or evaluation of the subject matter against the criteria, such as measurement uncertainty. See paragraphs 4.32–.34 and 5.59 for example language.]

[Additional paragraph(s) may be added to emphasize certain matters relating to the examination engagement or the subject matter. See paragraph 4.35.]

In our opinion, the schedule of greenhouse gas emissions of XYZ Company for *[identify the period, for example, the year ended December 31, 20XX]* is presented in accordance with *[identify criteria]*, in all material respects.

[Practitioner's signature]
[Practitioner's city and state]
[Date of practitioner's report]

Example 4: Practitioner's Examination Report on Management's Assertion About Specified Indicators; Unmodified Conclusion

See paragraphs 4.42–.43 when the practitioner's opinion is modified. This illustrative report also contains additional language regarding management's responsibilities that may be included in the report (the language is shown in brackets).

Independent Accountant's Report

[Appropriate Addressee]

We have examined management of XYZ Company's assertion that *[identify the assertion, including the subject matter and the criteria, for example, the selected sustainability metrics identified below and denoted by an asterisk (*) within the accompanying XYZ Company Corporate Responsibility Report, as of and for the periods indicated below, are presented in accordance with the criteria set forth in the accompanying management assertion.]*

[*List the applicable sustainability metrics and the date or period (for example:*

- *Ethnic diversity—United States—as of November 30, 20X0*
- *Recordable incidence rate—United States, Canada and Mexico—year ended December 31, 20X0*
- *Foundation grant-making—year ended December 31, 20X0*
- *Greenhouse gas emissions—Scope 1 and Scope 2—year ended December 31, 20X0*
- *Water use—year ended December 31, 20X0)]*

XYZ Company's management is responsible for its assertion [and for the selection (or development) of the criteria, which management believes provide an objective basis for measuring and reporting on the selected sustainability metrics. Management is also responsible for designing, implementing, and maintaining internal control relevant to the preparation and presentation of the selected sustainability metrics to prevent, or detect and correct, misstatement of the selected sustainability metrics, whether due to fraud or error]. Our responsibility is to express an opinion on management's assertion based on our examination.

Our examination was conducted in accordance with attestation standards established by the American Institute of Certified Public Accountants. Those standards require that we plan and perform the examination to obtain reasonable assurance about whether management's assertion is fairly stated, in all material respects. An examination involves performing procedures to obtain evidence about management's assertion. The nature, timing, and extent of the procedures selected depend on our judgment, including an assessment of the risks of material misstatement of management's assertion, whether due to fraud or error. We believe that the evidence we obtained is sufficient and appropriate to provide a reasonable basis for our opinion.

[*Include a description of significant inherent limitations, if any, associated with the measurement or evaluation of the subject matter against the criteria, such as measurement uncertainty. See paragraphs 4.32–.34 and 5.59 for example language.*]

[*Additional paragraph(s) may be added to emphasize certain matters relating to the examination engagement or the subject matter. See paragraph 4.35.*]

In our opinion, management's assertion that [*identify the assertion, including the subject matter and the criteria, for example, the selected sustainability metrics identified above are presented in accordance with (identify criteria; for example, the criteria set forth in the accompanying management assertion)*] is fairly stated, in all material respects.

[*Practitioner's signature*]
[*Practitioner's city and state*]
[*Date of practitioner's report*]

Example 5: Practitioner's Examination Report on Management's Assertion About GHG Emissions Information; Unmodified Opinion

See paragraphs 4.42–.43 when the practitioner's opinion is modified.

Independent Accountant's Report

[*Appropriate Addressee*]

We have examined management of XYZ Company's assertion that [*identify the assertion, for example, the accompanying schedule of greenhouse gas emissions for XYZ Company for the year ended December 31, 20XX, is presented in accordance with (identify criteria)*]. XYZ Company's management is responsible for its assertion. Our responsibility is to express an opinion on management's assertion based on our examination.

Our examination was conducted in accordance with attestation standards established by the American Institute of Certified Public Accountants. Those standards require that we plan and perform the examination to obtain reasonable assurance about whether management's assertion is fairly stated, in all material respects. An examination involves performing procedures to obtain evidence about management's assertion. The nature, timing, and extent of the procedures selected depend on our judgment, including an assessment of the risks of material misstatement of management's assertion, whether due to fraud or error. We believe that the evidence we obtained is sufficient and appropriate to provide a reasonable basis for our opinion.

[*Include a description of significant inherent limitations, if any, associated with the measurement or evaluation of the subject matter against the criteria, such as measurement uncertainty. See paragraphs 4.32–.34 and 5.59 for example language.*]

[*Additional paragraph(s) may be added to emphasize certain matters relating to the examination engagement or the subject matter. See paragraph 4.35.*]

In our opinion, management's assertion that [*identify the assertion, including the subject matter and the criteria, for example, the accompanying schedule of greenhouse gas emissions for XYZ Company for the year ended December 31, 20XX, is presented in accordance with (identify criteria)*] is fairly stated, in all material respects.

[*Practitioner's signature*]

[*Practitioner's city and state*]

[*Date of practitioner's report*]

Example 6: Practitioner's Examination Report on GHG Emissions Information; Practitioner Makes Reference to the Examination Report of an Other Practitioner on a Component Entity; Reporting on the Subject Matter; Unmodified Opinion

Independent Accountant's Report

[*Appropriate Addressee*]

We have examined the accompanying schedule of greenhouse gas emissions of XYZ Company and subsidiaries for the year ended

Illustrative Practitioner's Examination Reports

December 31, 20XX. XYZ Company's management is responsible for preparing and presenting the schedule in accordance with [*identify the criteria*]. Our responsibility is to express an opinion on the schedule of greenhouse gas emissions based on our examination. We did not examine the schedule of greenhouse gas emissions for ABC Company, a wholly owned subsidiary, for which emissions represented 20 percent of the related consolidated emissions for the year ended December 31, 20XX. This schedule was examined by other accountants, whose report has been furnished to us and our opinion, insofar as it relates to the amounts included for ABC Company, is based solely on the report of the other accountants.

Our examination was conducted in accordance with attestation standards established by the American Institute of Certified Public Accountants. Those standards require that we plan and perform the examination to obtain reasonable assurance about whether the schedule of greenhouse gas emissions is presented in accordance with the criteria, in all material respects. An examination involves performing procedures to obtain evidence about [*identify the subject matter, for example, the schedule of greenhouse gas emissions*]. The nature, timing, and extent of the procedures selected depend on our judgment, including an assessment of the risks of material misstatement of the schedule of greenhouse gas emissions, whether due to fraud or error. We believe that the evidence we obtained, including the report of the other accountants, is sufficient and appropriate to provide a reasonable basis for our opinion.

[*Include a description of significant inherent limitations, if any, associated with the measurement or evaluation of the subject matter against the criteria, such as measurement uncertainty. See paragraphs 4.32–.34 and 5.59 for example language.*]

[*Additional paragraph(s) may be added to emphasize certain matters relating to the examination engagement or the subject matter. See paragraph 4.35.*]

In our opinion, based on our examination and the report of the other accountants, the accompanying schedule of greenhouse gas emissions of XYZ Company for the year ended December 31, 20XX, is presented in accordance with [*identify criteria*], in all material respects.

[*Practitioner's signature*]

[*Practitioner's city and state*]

[*Date of practitioner's report*]

Example 7: Practitioner's Examination Report on GHG Emission Reduction Information Related to a Specific Project; Reporting on the Subject Matter; Unmodified Opinion

Independent Accountant's Report

[*Appropriate Addressee*]

We have examined the accompanying schedule of reductions of greenhouse gas emissions of XYZ Company related to the ABC project for the year ended December 31, 20XX, from its GHG emissions in the prior year. XYZ Company's management is responsible for preparing and presenting the schedule in accordance with [*identify the criteria*].

Our responsibility is to express an opinion on the schedule of reductions of greenhouse gas emissions based on our examination.

Our examination was conducted in accordance with attestation standards established by the American Institute of Certified Public Accountants. Those standards require that we plan and perform the examination to obtain reasonable assurance about whether the schedule of reductions of greenhouse gas emissions is presented in accordance with the criteria, in all material respects. An examination involves performing procedures to obtain evidence about [*identify the subject matter, for example, the schedule of reductions of greenhouse gas emissions*]. The nature, timing, and extent of the procedures selected depend on our judgment, including an assessment of the risks of material misstatement of the schedule of reductions of greenhouse gas emissions, whether due to fraud or error. We believe that the evidence we obtained is sufficient and appropriate to provide a reasonable basis for our opinion.

[*Include a description of significant inherent limitations, if any, associated with the measurement or evaluation of the subject matter against the criteria, such as measurement uncertainty. See paragraphs 4.32–.34 and 5.59 for example language.*]

[*Additional paragraph(s) may be added to emphasize certain matters relating to the examination engagement or the subject matter. See paragraph 4.35.*]

Our report relates to the ABC project identified above. We were not engaged to, and did not, examine XYZ Company's entity-wide greenhouse gas emissions inventory or whether XYZ Company has reduced its entity-wide greenhouse gas emissions inventory. Accordingly, we do not express an opinion or any other form of assurance on its entity-wide greenhouse gas emissions inventory or changes from prior periods.

In our opinion, the schedule of reductions of greenhouse gas emissions of XYZ Company related to ABC project for the year ended December 31, 20XX is presented in accordance with [*identify criteria*], in all material respects.

[*Practitioner's signature*]

[*Practitioner's city and state*]

[*Date of practitioner's report*]

Example 8: Practitioner's Examination Report on Management's Assertion About GHG Emission Reduction Information; Unmodified Opinion

See paragraphs 4.42–.43 when the practitioner's opinion is modified.

Independent Accountant's Report

[*Appropriate Addressee*]

We have examined management of XYZ Company's assertion that [*identify the assertion, for example, XYZ Company reduced GHG emissions in connection with project ABC by 50,000 tons of CO2 equivalents for the year ended December 31, 20XX, from its GHG emissions in the prior year*] based on [*identify criteria selected by management*]. XYZ

Company's management is responsible for its assertion. Our responsibility is to express an opinion on management's assertion based on our examination.

Our examination was conducted in accordance with attestation standards established by the American Institute of Certified Public Accountants. Those standards require that we plan and perform the examination to obtain reasonable assurance about whether management's assertion is fairly stated, in all material respects. An examination involves performing procedures to obtain evidence about management's assertion. The nature, timing, and extent of the procedures selected depend on our judgment, including an assessment of the risks of material misstatement of management's assertion, whether due to fraud or error. We believe that the evidence we obtained is sufficient and appropriate to provide a reasonable basis for our opinion.

[Include a description of significant inherent limitations, if any, associated with the measurement or evaluation of the subject matter against the criteria, such as measurement uncertainty. See paragraphs 4.32–.34 and 5.59 for example language.]

[Additional paragraph(s) may be added to emphasize certain matters relating to the examination engagement or the subject matter. See paragraph 4.35.]

Our engagement related to the specific project identified above. We were not engaged to, and did not, examine XYZ Company's entity-wide greenhouse gas emissions inventory or whether XYZ Company has reduced its entity-wide greenhouse gas emissions inventory. Accordingly, we do not express an opinion or any other form of assurance on its entity-wide greenhouse gas emissions inventory or changes from prior periods.

In our opinion, management's assertion that [identify the assertion, including the subject matter and the criteria, for example, XYZ Company reduced GHG emissions in connection with project ABC by 50,000 tons of CO2 equivalents for the year ended December 31, 20XX, from its GHG emissions in the prior year] based on [identify criteria selected by management] is fairly stated, in all material respects.

[Practitioner's signature]

[Practitioner's city and state]

[Date of practitioner's report]

Example 9: Practitioner's Examination Report on GHG Emissions Information; Reporting on the Subject Matter; Qualified Opinion

Independent Accountant's Report

[Appropriate Addressee]

We have examined the accompanying schedule of greenhouse gas emissions of XYZ Company for [identify the period, for example, the year ended December 31, 20XX]. XYZ Company's management is responsible for preparing and presenting the schedule of greenhouse gas emissions in accordance with [identify the criteria]. Our responsibility is to express an opinion on the schedule of greenhouse gas emissions based on our examination.

Our examination was conducted in accordance with attestation standards established by the American Institute of Certified Public Accountants. Those standards require that we plan and perform the examination to obtain reasonable assurance about whether the schedule of greenhouse gas emissions is presented in accordance with the criteria, in all material respects. An examination involves performing procedures to obtain evidence about [*identify the subject matter, for example, the schedule of greenhouse gas emissions*]. The nature, timing, and extent of the procedures selected depend on our judgment, including an assessment of the risks of material misstatement of the schedule of greenhouse gas emissions, whether due to fraud or error. We believe that the evidence we obtained is sufficient and appropriate to provide a reasonable basis for our opinion.

[*Include a description of significant inherent limitations, if any, associated with the measurement or evaluation of the subject matter against the criteria, such as measurement uncertainty. See paragraphs 4.32–.34 and 5.59 for example language.*]

[*Additional paragraph(s) may be added to emphasize certain matters relating to the examination engagement or the subject matter. See paragraph 4.35.*]

Our examination disclosed that [*describe condition(s) that, individually or in the aggregate, resulted in a material misstatement or deviation from the criteria; for example, greenhouse gas emissions information for Subsidiary X was excluded from the schedule of greenhouse gas emissions; such subsidiary represents X% of the consolidated (assets, revenues or other key element)*].

In our opinion, except for the material misstatement [*or deviation from the criteria*] described in the preceding paragraph, the schedule of greenhouse gas emissions of XYZ Company for [*identify the period, for example, the year ended December 31, 20XX*] is presented in accordance with [*identify criteria*], in all material respects.

[*Practitioner's signature*]

[*Practitioner's city and state*]

[*Date of practitioner's report*]

Appendix E

Illustrative Practitioner's Review Reports

This appendix is nonauthoritative and is included for informational purposes only.

The illustrative review reports included in this appendix are provided for a few of the common reporting situations that a practitioner might encounter with respect to sustainability information but are not intended to be a complete list. These reports are intended for general use situations. See paragraphs .47–.49 of AT-C section 210, *Review Engagements* (AICPA, *Professional Standards*), for requirements and guidance on restricting the use of a review report.

> Example 1: Practitioner's Review Report on an Entire Sustainability Report; Reporting on the Subject Matter; Unmodified Conclusion
>
> Example 2: Practitioner's Review Report on Specified Indicators; Reporting on the Subject Matter; Unmodified Conclusion
>
> Example 3: Practitioner's Review Report on GHG Emissions Information; Reporting on the Subject Matter; Unmodified Conclusion
>
> Example 4: Practitioner's Review Report on Management's Assertion About Specified Indicators; Unmodified Conclusion
>
> Example 5: Practitioner's Review Report on Management's Assertion About GHG Emissions Information; Unmodified Conclusion
>
> Example 6: Practitioner's Review Report on GHG Emissions Information; Practitioner Makes Reference to the Review Report of an Other Practitioner on a Component of the Entity; Reporting on the Subject Matter; Unmodified Conclusion
>
> Example 7: Practitioner's Review Report on GHG Emission Reduction Information Related to a Specific Project; Reporting on the Subject Matter; Unmodified Conclusion
>
> Example 8: Practitioner's Review Report on Management's Assertion About GHG Emission Reduction Information; Unmodified Conclusion
>
> Example 9: Practitioner's Review Report on GHG Emissions Information; Reporting on the Subject Matter; Qualified Conclusion

Example 1: Practitioner's Review Report on an Entire Sustainability Report; Reporting on the Subject Matter; Unmodified Conclusion

An illustrative concluding paragraph is also illustrated below for when the subject matter is a specified section of a sustainability report.

Independent Accountant's Review Report

[*Appropriate Addressee*]

We have reviewed [*identify the subject matter, for example, the sustainability report of XYZ Company for the year ended December 31,*

20XX]. XYZ Company's management is responsible for preparing and presenting [*identify the subject matter, for example, the sustainability report*] in accordance with [*identify the criteria, for example, ABC criteria as further described [on pages X-X of the sustainability report]/[in the accompanying notes]*]. Our responsibility is to express a conclusion on [*identify the subject matter, for example, the sustainability report*] based on our review.

Our review was conducted in accordance with attestation standards established by the American Institute of Certified Public Accountants. Those standards require that we plan and perform the review to obtain limited assurance about whether any material modifications should be made to [*identify the subject matter, for example, the sustainability report*] in order for it to be [presented][1] in accordance with the criteria. A review is substantially less in scope than an examination, the objective of which is to obtain reasonable assurance about whether [*identify the subject matter, for example, the sustainability report*] is [presented][2] in accordance with the criteria, in all material respects, in order to express an opinion. Accordingly, we do not express such an opinion. We believe that our review provides a reasonable basis for our conclusion.

[*Include a description of significant inherent limitations, if any, associated with the measurement or evaluation of the subject matter against the criteria, such as measurement uncertainty. See paragraphs 4.32–.34 and 5.59 for illustrative language.*]

[*Additional paragraph(s) may be added to emphasize certain matters relating to the review engagement or the subject matter. See paragraph 4.35.*]

Based on our review, we are not aware of any material modifications that should be made to [*identify the subject matter, for example, the accompanying sustainability report of XYZ Company for the year ended December 31, 20XX*], in order for it to be [presented][3] in accordance with [*identify the criteria, for example, ABC criteria as further described [on pages X to X of the sustainability report]/[in the accompanying notes]*].

[*Practitioner's signature*]
[*Practitioner's city and state*]
[*Date of practitioner's report*]

---

[1] Typically, sustainability information is in the form of a presentation and, accordingly, references might be to "presented in accordance with" as opposed to "in accordance with." Whichever wording is selected, it should be used consistently between the scope paragraph and the concluding paragraph (that is, if the scope paragraph refers to "presented in accordance with," then the concluding paragraph should use "presented in accordance with"). This applies to all subsequent references in this appendix to "presented in accordance with."

[2] Refer to footnote 1 in example 1 of this appendix for detailed guidance.

[3] Refer to footnote 1 in example 1 of this appendix for detailed guidance.

Example 2: Practitioner's Review Report on Specified Indicators; Reporting on the Subject Matter; Unmodified Conclusion

An illustrative concluding paragraph is also illustrated below for when the subject matter is a specified section of a sustainability report.

Independent Accountant's Review Report

[*Appropriate Addressee*]

We have reviewed [*identify the subject matter, for example, the following specified indicators included in XYZ Company's sustainability report for the year ended December 31, 20XX*].

- [*Indicator 1*]
- [*Indicator 2*]

XYZ Company's management is responsible for [*identify the subject matter, for example, preparing and presenting the above specified indicators*] in accordance with [*identify the criteria, for example, the criteria specified on page XX of the accompanying sustainability report*]. Our responsibility is to express a conclusion on [*identify the subject matter, for example, the specified indicators*] based on our review.

Our review was conducted in accordance with attestation standards established by the American Institute of Certified Public Accountants. Those standards require that we plan and perform the review to obtain limited assurance about whether any material modifications should be made to [*identify the subject matter, for example, the specified indicators*] in order for them/it to be [presented][4] in accordance with the criteria. A review is substantially less in scope than an examination, the objective of which is to obtain reasonable assurance about whether [*identify the subject matter, for example, the specified indicators*] are/is [presented][5] in accordance with the criteria, in all material respects, in order to express an opinion. Accordingly, we do not express such an opinion. We believe that our review provides a reasonable basis for our conclusion.

[*Include a description of significant inherent limitations, if any, associated with the measurement or evaluation of the subject matter against the criteria, such as measurement uncertainty. See paragraphs 4.32–.34 and 5.59 for illustrative language.*]

[*Additional paragraph(s) may be added to emphasize certain matters relating to the review engagement or the subject matter. See paragraph 4.35.*]

Based our review, we are not aware of any material modifications that should be made to [*identify the subject matter, for example, the specified indicators referred to above*] in order for them/it to be [presented][6] in

---

[4] Refer to footnote 1 in example 1 of this appendix for detailed guidance.
[5] Refer to footnote 1 in example 1 of this appendix for detailed guidance.
[6] Refer to footnote 1 in example 1 of this appendix for detailed guidance.

accordance with [*identify the criteria, for example, the criteria specified within the report*].

[*Practitioner's signature*]
[*Practitioner's city and state*]
[*Date of practitioner's report*]

Conclusion paragraph covering a specified section of a sustainability report:

> Based our review, we are not aware of any material modifications that should be made to [*identify the subject matter, for example, specify the applicable section*] of [*identify the report that the subject matter is included in, for example, the 20XX sustainability report of XYZ Company*] in order for it to be [presented][7] in accordance with [*identify the criteria*].

Depending on the nature of, and information included in, the specified section, the following might be an appropriate alternative:

> Based our review, we are not aware of any material modifications that should be made to [*specify the subject matter section*] in the accompanying [*identify the report that the subject matter is included in, for example, the 20XX sustainability report of XYZ Company*] in order for it to be [presented][8] in accordance with [*identify the criteria*], in all material respects.

Example 3: Practitioner's Review Report on GHG Emissions Information; Reporting on the Subject Matter; Unmodified Conclusion

Independent Accountant's Report

[*Appropriate Addressee*]

We have reviewed the accompanying schedule of greenhouse gas emissions of XYZ Company for [*identify period, for example, the year ended December 31, 20XX*]. XYZ Company's management is responsible for preparing and presenting the schedule of greenhouse gas emissions in accordance with [*identify the criteria*]. Our responsibility is to express a conclusion on the schedule of greenhouse gas emissions based on our review.

Our review was conducted in accordance with attestation standards established by the American Institute of Certified Public Accountants. Those standards require that we plan and perform our review to obtain limited assurance about whether any material modifications should be made to the schedule of greenhouse gas emissions in order for it to be [presented][9] in accordance with the criteria. A review is substantially less in scope than an examination, the objective of which is to obtain reasonable assurance about whether the schedule of greenhouse gas emissions is [presented][10] in accordance with the criteria, in all material respects, in order to express an opinion. Accordingly, we do not

---

[7] Refer to footnote 1 in example 1 of this appendix for detailed guidance.
[8] Refer to footnote 1 in example 1 of this appendix for detailed guidance.
[9] Refer to footnote 1 in example 1 of this appendix for detailed guidance.
[10] Refer to footnote 1 in example 1 of this appendix for detailed guidance.

express such an opinion. We believe that our review provides a reasonable basis for our conclusion.

[*Include a description of significant inherent limitations, if any, associated with the measurement or evaluation of the subject matter against the criteria, such as measurement uncertainty. See paragraphs 4.32–.34 and 5.59 for example language.*]

[*Additional paragraph(s) may be added to emphasize certain matters relating to the review engagement or the subject matter. See paragraph 4.35.*]

Based on our review, we are not aware of any material modifications that should be made to the schedule referred to above in order for it to be [presented][11] in accordance with [*identify criteria*].

[*Practitioner's signature*]
[*Practitioner's city and state*]
[*Date of practitioner's report*]

Example 4: Practitioner's Review Report on Management's Assertion About Specified Indicators; Unmodified Conclusion

See paragraphs 4.44–.45 for modifications to the practitioner's report when the practitioner's conclusion is modified. This illustrative report also contains additional language regarding management's responsibilities that may be included in the report (the language is shown in brackets).

Independent Accountant's Review Report

[*Appropriate Addressee*]

We have reviewed management of XYZ Company's assertion that [*identify the assertion, including the subject matter and the criteria, for example, the selected sustainability metrics identified below and denoted by an asterisk (*) within the accompanying XYZ Company Corporate Responsibility Report, as of and for the periods indicated below, are [presented]*][12] *in accordance with the criteria set forth in the accompanying management assertion.*]

[*List the applicable sustainability metrics and the date or period (for example:*

- *Ethnic diversity—United States—as of November 30, 20X0*
- *Recordable incidence rate—United States, Canada and Mexico—year ended December 31, 20X0*
- *Foundation grantmaking—year ended December 31, 20X0*
- *Greenhouse gas emissions—Scope 1 and Scope 2—year ended December 31, 20X0*
- *Water use—year ended December 31, 20X0)*]

---

[11] Refer to footnote 1 in example 1 of this appendix for detailed guidance.

[12] Typically, sustainability information is in the form of a presentation and, accordingly, management might make an assertion that the sustainability information is "presented in accordance with" the identified criteria. If management's assertion uses "presented," then the practitioner's report also should use "presented." Refer to paragraph 4.19 for guidance regarding the use of "presented."

XYZ Company's management is responsible for its assertion [and for the selection (or development) of the criteria, which management believes provide an objective basis for measuring and reporting on the selected sustainability metrics. Management is also responsible for designing, implementing, and maintaining internal control relevant to the preparation and presentation of the selected sustainability metrics to prevent, or detect and correct, misstatement of the selected sustainability metrics, whether due to fraud or error]. Our responsibility is to express a conclusion on management's assertion based on our review.

Our review was conducted in accordance with attestation standards established by the American Institute of Certified Public Accountants. Those standards require that we plan and perform the review to obtain limited assurance about whether any material modifications should be made to management's assertion in order for it to be fairly stated. A review is substantially less in scope than an examination, the objective of which is to obtain reasonable assurance about whether management's assertion is fairly stated, in all material respects, in order to express an opinion. Accordingly, we do not express such an opinion. We believe that our review provides a reasonable basis for our conclusion.

[Include a description of significant inherent limitations, if any, associated with the measurement or evaluation of the subject matter against the criteria, such as measurement uncertainty. See paragraphs 4.32–.34 and 5.59 for illustrative language.]

[Additional paragraph(s) may be added to emphasize certain matters relating to the review engagement or the subject matter. See paragraph 4.35.]

Based on our review, we are not aware of any material modifications that should be made to management of XYZ Company's assertion in order for it to be fairly stated.

[Practitioner's signature]
[Practitioner's city and state]
[Date of practitioner's report]

Example 5: Practitioner's Review Report on Management's Assertion About GHG Emissions Information; Unmodified Conclusion

See paragraphs 4.44–.45 for modifications to the practitioner's report when the practitioner's conclusion is modified. This illustrative report also contains additional language regarding management's responsibilities that may be included in the report (the language is shown in brackets).

Independent Accountant's Report

[Appropriate Addressee]

We have reviewed management's assertion that [identify the assertion, including the subject matter and the criteria, for example, the accompanying schedule of greenhouse gas emissions of XYZ Company for the year ended December 31, 20XX, is [presented][13] in accordance with (identify criteria)]. XYZ Company's management is responsible for its

---

[13] Refer to footnote 12 in example 4 of this appendix for detailed guidance.

assertion [and for the selection (or development) of the criteria, which management believes provide an objective basis for measuring and reporting on the greenhouse gas emissions. Management is also responsible for designing, implementing, and maintaining internal control relevant to the preparation and presentation of the schedule of greenhouse gas emissions to prevent or detect and correct, misstatement, whether due to fraud or error]. Our responsibility is to express a conclusion on management's assertion based on our review.

Our review was conducted in accordance with attestation standards established by the American Institute of Certified Public Accountants. Those standards require that we plan and perform the review to obtain limited assurance about whether any material modifications should be made to management's assertion in order for it to be fairly stated. A review is substantially less in scope than an examination, the objective of which is to obtain reasonable assurance about whether management's assertion is fairly stated, in all material respects, in order to express an opinion. Accordingly, we do not express such an opinion. We believe that our review provides a reasonable basis for our conclusion.

[Include a description of significant inherent limitations, if any, associated with the measurement or evaluation of the subject matter against the criteria, such as measurement uncertainty. See paragraphs 4.32–.34 and 5.59 for illustrative language.]

[Additional paragraph(s) may be added to emphasize certain matters relating to the review engagement or the subject matter. See paragraph 4.35.]

Based on our review, we are not aware of any material modifications that should be made to management of XZY Company's assertion in order for it to be fairly stated.

[Practitioner's signature]
[Practitioner's city and state]
[Date of practitioner's report]

Example 6: Practitioner's Review Report on GHG Emissions Information; Practitioner Makes Reference to the Review Report of an Other Practitioner on a Component of the Entity; Reporting on the Subject Matter; Unmodified Conclusion

Independent Accountant's Report

[Appropriate Addressee]

We have reviewed the accompanying schedule of greenhouse gas emissions of XYZ Company and subsidiaries for the year ended December 31, 20XX. XYZ Company's management is responsible for preparing and presenting the schedule of greenhouse gas emissions in accordance with [identify the criteria]. Our responsibility is to express a conclusion on the schedule of greenhouse gas emissions based on our review. We did not review the schedule of greenhouse gas emissions of ABC Company, a wholly owned subsidiary, for which emissions represented 20 percent of the related consolidated emissions for the year ended December 31, 20XX. That schedule was reviewed by other accountants, whose report has been furnished to us, and our conclusion, insofar as it relates to the amounts included for ABC Company, is based solely on the report of the other accountants.

Our review was conducted in accordance with attestation standards established by the American Institute of Certified Public Accountants. Those standards require that we plan and perform the review to obtain limited assurance about whether any material modifications should be made to the schedule of greenhouse gas emissions in order for it to be [presented][14] in accordance with the criteria. A review is substantially less in scope than an examination, the objective of which is to obtain reasonable assurance about whether the schedule of greenhouse gas emissions is [presented][15] in accordance with the criteria, in all material respects, in order to express an opinion. Accordingly, we do not express such an opinion. We believe that our review and the report of the other accountants provide a reasonable basis for our conclusion.

[Include a description of significant inherent limitations, if any, associated with the measurement or evaluation of the subject matter against the criteria, such as measurement uncertainty. See paragraphs 4.32–.34 and 5.59 for example language.]

[Additional paragraph(s) may be added to emphasize certain matters relating to the review engagement or the subject matter. See paragraph 4.35.]

Based on our review and the review report of the other accountants, we are not aware of any material modifications that should be made to the schedule referred to above in order for it to be [presented][16] in accordance with [identify criteria].

[Practitioner's signature]
[Practitioner's city and state]
[Date of practitioner's report]

Example 7: Practitioner's Review Report on GHG Emission Reduction Information Related to a Specific Project; Reporting on the Subject Matter; Unmodified Conclusion

Independent Accountant's Report

[Appropriate Addressee]

We have reviewed the accompanying schedule of reductions of greenhouse gas emissions of XYZ Company related to the ABC project for the year ended December 31, 20XX, from its GHG emissions in the prior year. XYZ Company's management is responsible for preparing and presenting the schedule of reductions of greenhouse gas emissions in accordance with [identify the criteria]. Our responsibility is to express a conclusion on the schedule of greenhouse gas emissions based on our review.

---

[14] Refer to footnote 1 in example 1 of this appendix for detailed guidance.
[15] Refer to footnote 1 in example 1 of this appendix for detailed guidance.
[16] Refer to footnote 1 in example 1 of this appendix for detailed guidance.

Illustrative Practitioner's Review Reports

Our review was conducted in accordance with attestation standards established by the American Institute of Certified Public Accountants. Those standards require that we plan and perform the review to obtain limited assurance about whether any material modifications should be made to the schedule of reductions of greenhouse gas emissions in order for it to be [presented][17] in accordance with the criteria. A review is substantially less in scope than an examination, the objective of which is to obtain reasonable assurance about whether the schedule of reductions of greenhouse gas emissions is [presented][18] in accordance with the criteria, in all material respects, in order to express an opinion. Accordingly, we do not express such an opinion. We believe that our review provides a reasonable basis for our conclusion.

[Include a description of significant inherent limitations, if any, associated with the measurement or evaluation of the subject matter against the criteria, such as measurement uncertainty. See paragraphs 4.32–.34 and 5.59 for illustrative language.]

[Additional paragraph(s) may be added to emphasize certain matters relating to the review engagement or the subject matter. See paragraph 4.35.]

Our report relates to the ABC project identified above. We were not engaged to, and did not, review XYZ Company's entity-wide greenhouse gas emissions inventory or whether XYZ Company has reduced its entity-wide greenhouse gas emissions inventory. Accordingly, we do not express any conclusion on its entity-wide greenhouse gas emissions inventory or changes from prior periods.

Based on our review, we are not aware of any material modifications that should be made to the schedule of reductions of greenhouse gas emissions of XYZ Company related to ABC project for the year ended December 31, 20XX, in order for it to be [presented][19] in accordance with [identify criteria].

[Practitioner's signature]
[Practitioner's city and state]
[Date of practitioner's report]

Example 8: Practitioner's Review Report on Management's Assertion About GHG Emission Reduction Information; Unmodified Conclusion

The following is an illustrative practitioner's review report for an engagement in which the practitioner has reviewed management's assertion about a schedule of reductions of an entity's greenhouse gas emissions and is reporting on that assertion. See paragraphs 4.44–.45 when the practitioner's conclusion is modified.

---

[17] Refer to footnote 1 in example 1 of this appendix for detailed guidance.
[18] Refer to footnote 1 in example 1 of this appendix for detailed guidance.
[19] Refer to footnote 1 in example 1 of this appendix for detailed guidance.

Independent Accountant's Report

[Appropriate Addressee]

We have reviewed management's assertion that [identify the assertion, including the subject matter and the criteria, for example, XYZ Company reduced GHG emissions in connection with project ABC by 50,000 tons of CO2 equivalents for the year ended December 31, 20XX from its GHG emissions in the prior year based on ABC criteria]. XYZ Company's management is responsible for its assertion. Our responsibility is to express a conclusion on management's assertion based on our review.

Our review was conducted in accordance with attestation standards established by the American Institute of Certified Public Accountants. Those standards require that we plan and perform the review to obtain limited assurance about whether any material modifications should be made to management's assertion in order for it to be fairly stated. A review is substantially less in scope than an examination, the objective of which is to obtain reasonable assurance about whether management's assertion is fairly stated, in all material respects, in order to express an opinion on management's assertion. Accordingly, we do not express such an opinion. We believe that our review provides a reasonable basis for our conclusion.

[Include a description of significant inherent limitations, if any, associated with the measurement or evaluation of the subject matter against the criteria, such as measurement uncertainty. See paragraphs 4.32–.34 and 5.59 for illustrative language.]

[Additional paragraph(s) may be added to emphasize certain matters relating to the review engagement or the subject matter. See paragraph 4.35.]

Based on our review, we are not aware of any material modifications that should be made to management's assertion that [identify the assertion, for example, XYZ Company reduced GHG emissions in connection with project ABC by 50,000 tons of CO2 equivalents for the year ended December 31, 20XX from its GHG emissions in the prior year] based on [identify criteria selected by management] in order for it to be fairly stated.

[Practitioner's signature]
[Practitioner's city and state]
[Date of practitioner's report]

Example 9: Practitioner's Review Report on GHG Emissions Information; Reporting on the Subject Matter; Qualified Conclusion

Independent Accountant's Report

[Appropriate Addressee]

We have reviewed the accompanying schedule of greenhouse gas emissions of XYZ Company for [identify the period, for example, the year ended December 31, 20XX]. XYZ Company's management is responsible for preparing and presenting the schedule of greenhouse gas emissions in accordance with [identify the criteria]. Our responsibility is

Illustrative Practitioner's Review Reports

to express a conclusion on the schedule of greenhouse gas emissions based on our review.

Our review was conducted in accordance with attestation standards established by the American Institute of Certified Public Accountants. Those standards require that we plan and perform the review to obtain limited assurance about whether any material modifications should be made to the schedule of greenhouse gas emissions in order for it to be [presented][20] in accordance with the criteria. A review is substantially less in scope than an examination, the objective of which is to obtain reasonable assurance about whether the schedule of greenhouse gas emissions is [presented][21] in accordance with the criteria, in all material respects, in order to express an opinion. Accordingly, we do not express such an opinion. We believe that our review provides a reasonable basis for our conclusion.

[Include a description of significant inherent limitations, if any, associated with the measurement or evaluation of the subject matter against the criteria, such as measurement uncertainty. See paragraphs 4.32–.34 and 5.59 for example language.]

[Additional paragraph(s) may be added to emphasize certain matters relating to the examination engagement or the subject matter. See paragraph 4.35.]

Our review identified that [describe condition(s) that, individually or in the aggregate, resulted in a material misstatement or deviation from the criteria; for example, greenhouse gas emissions information for Subsidiary X was excluded from the schedule of greenhouse gas emissions; such subsidiary represents X% of the consolidated [identify assets, revenues or other key element]].

Based on our review, except for the matter(s) described in the preceding paragraph, we are not aware of any material modifications that should be made to the schedule referred to above in order for it to be [presented][22] in accordance with [identify criteria].

[Practitioner's signature]
[Practitioner's city and state]
[Date of practitioner's report]

---

[20] Refer to footnote 1 in example 1 of this appendix for detailed guidance.
[21] Refer to footnote 1 in example 1 of this appendix for detailed guidance.
[22] Refer to footnote 1 in example 1 of this appendix for detailed guidance.

Appendix F

Illustrative Practitioner's Report on an Examination of One or More Specified Indicators and a Review of Others, Reporting on the Subject Matter, Unmodified Opinion and Unmodified Conclusion

This appendix is nonauthoritative and is included for informational purposes only.

The following is an illustrative practitioner's single report for an engagement in which the practitioner has examined certain sustainability information and reviewed other sustainability information and is reporting on the sustainability information in a single report as permitted by AT-C sections 205, *Examination Engagements*, and 210, *Review Engagements* (AICPA, *Professional Standards*).[1]

Independent Accountant's Report

[*Appropriate Addressee*]

EXAMINATION OF CERTAIN SUSTAINABILITY INFORMATION

We have examined [*identify the subject matter, for example, the following specified indicators included in XYZ Company's sustainability report for the year ended December 31, 20XX*]:

- [*Indicator 1*]
- [*Indicator 2*]

XYZ Company's management is responsible for preparing and presenting [*identify the subject matter, for example, the above specified indicators*] in accordance with [*identify the criteria, for example, the criteria specified on page XX of the accompanying sustainability report*]. Our responsibility is to express an opinion on these [*identify the subject matter, for example, the specified indicators*] based on our examination.

Our examination was conducted in accordance with attestation standards established by the American Institute of Certified Public Accountants. Those standards require that we plan and perform the examination to obtain reasonable assurance about whether [*identify the subject matter, for example, the specified indicators listed above*] are/is presented in accordance with the criteria, in all material respects. An examination involves performing procedures to obtain evidence about [*identify the subject matter, for example, the specified indicators listed above*]. The nature, timing, and extent of the procedures selected depend on our judgment, including an assessment of the risks of material misstatement of [*identify the subject matter, for example, the specified*

---

[1] See paragraph .A89 of AT-C section 205, *Examination Engagements*, and paragraph .A68 of AT-C section 210, *Review Engagements* (AICPA, *Professional Standards*).

indicators listed above], whether due to fraud or error. We believe that the evidence we obtained is sufficient and appropriate to provide a reasonable basis for our opinion.

[*Include a description of significant inherent limitations, if any, associated with the measurement or evaluation of the subject matter against the criteria, such as measurement uncertainty. See paragraphs 4.32–.34 and 5.59 for illustrative language.*]

[*Additional paragraph(s) may be added to emphasize certain matters relating to the review engagement or the subject matter. See paragraph 4.35.*]

In our opinion, [*identify the subject matter, for example, the specified indicators referred to above*] are/is presented in accordance with [*identify the criteria, for example, the criteria specified on page XX of the accompanying sustainability report*], in all material respects.

REVIEW OF CERTAIN SUSTAINABILITY INFORMATION

We have reviewed [*identify the subject matter, for example, the following specified indicators included in XYZ Company's sustainability report for the year ended December 31, 20XX*:]

- [*Indicator 3*]
- [*Indicator 4*]
- [*Indicator 5*]

XYZ Company's management is responsible for preparing and presenting [*identify the subject matter, for example, the above specified indicators*] in accordance with [*identify the criteria, for example, the criteria specified on page XX of the accompanying sustainability report*]. Our responsibility is to express a conclusion on these specified indicators based on our review.

Our review was conducted in accordance with attestation standards established by the American Institute of Certified Public Accountants. Those standards require that we plan and perform the review to obtain limited assurance about whether any material modifications should be made to [*identify the subject matter, for example, the specified indicators listed above*] in order for them/it to be presented in accordance with the criteria. A review is substantially less in scope than an examination, the objective of which is to obtain reasonable assurance about whether [*identify the subject matter, for example, the specified indicators*] are/is presented in accordance with the criteria, in all material respects in order to express an opinion. Accordingly, we do not express such an opinion. We believe that our review provides a reasonable basis for our conclusion.

[*Include a description of significant inherent limitations, if any, associated with the measurement or evaluation of the subject matter against the criteria, such as measurement uncertainty. See paragraphs 4.32–.34 and 5.59 for example language.*]

[*Additional paragraph(s) may be added to emphasize certain matters relating to the review engagement or the subject matter. See paragraph 4.35.*]

Based on our review, we are not aware of any material modifications that should be made to [*identify the subject matter, for example, the specified indicators listed above in XYZ Company's sustainability report for the year ended December 31, 20XX*], in order for [*identify the subject matter*] to be presented in accordance with [*identify the criteria, for example, the criteria specified on page XX of the accompanying sustainability report*].

[*Practitioner's signature*]
[*Practitioner's city and state*]
[*Date of practitioner's report*]

Appendix G

Overview of Statements on Quality Control Standards

This appendix is nonauthoritative and is included for informational purposes only.

This appendix is a partial reproduction of chapter 1 of the AICPA practice aid *Establishing and Maintaining a System of Quality Control for a CPA Firm's Accounting and Auditing Practice*, available at www.aicpa.org/interestareas/frc/pages/enhancingauditqualitypracticeaid.aspx.

This appendix highlights certain aspects of the quality control standards issued by the AICPA. If appropriate, readers should also refer to the quality control standards issued by the PCAOB, available at www.pcaobus.org/Standards/QC/Pages/default.aspx.

1.01 The objectives of a system of quality control are to provide a CPA firm with reasonable assurance[1] that the firm and its personnel comply with professional standards and applicable regulatory and legal requirements, and that the firm or engagement partners issue reports that are appropriate in the circumstances. QC section 10, *A Firm's System of Quality Control* (AICPA, *Professional Standards*), addresses a CPA firm's responsibilities for its system of quality control for its accounting and auditing practice. That section is to be read in conjunction with the AICPA Code of Professional Conduct and other relevant ethical requirements.

1.02 A system of quality control consists of policies designed to achieve the objectives of the system and the procedures necessary to implement and monitor compliance with those policies. The nature, extent, and formality of a firm's quality control policies and procedures will depend on various factors such as the firm's size; the number and operating characteristics of its offices; the degree of authority allowed to, and the knowledge and experience possessed by, firm personnel; and the nature and complexity of the firm's practice.

Communication of Quality Control Policies and Procedures

1.03 The firm should communicate its quality control policies and procedures to its personnel. Most firms will find it appropriate to communicate their policies and procedures in writing and distribute them, or make them available electronically, to all professional personnel. Effective communication includes the following:

- A description of quality control policies and procedures and the objectives they are designed to achieve
- The message that each individual has a personal responsibility for quality
- A requirement for each individual to be familiar with and to comply with these policies and procedures

---

[1] The term *reasonable assurance*, which is defined as a high, but not absolute, level of assurance, is used because absolute assurance cannot be attained. Paragraph .53 of QC section 10, *A Firm's System of Quality Control* (AICPA, *Professional Standards*), states, "Any system of quality control has inherent limitations that can reduce its effectiveness."

Effective communication also includes procedures for personnel to communicate their views or concerns on quality control matters to the firm's management.

Elements of a System of Quality Control

1.04 A firm must establish and maintain a system of quality control. The firm's system of quality control should include policies and procedures that address each of the following elements of quality control identified in paragraph .17 of QC section 10:

- Leadership responsibilities for quality within the firm (the "tone at the top")
- Relevant ethical requirements
- Acceptance and continuance of client relationships and specific engagements
- Human resources
- Engagement performance
- Monitoring

1.05 The elements of quality control are interrelated. For example, a firm continually assesses client relationships to comply with relevant ethical requirements, including independence, integrity, and objectivity, and policies and procedures related to the acceptance and continuance of client relationships and specific engagements. Similarly, the human resources element of quality control encompasses criteria related to professional development, hiring, advancement, and assignment of firm personnel to engagements, all of which affect policies and procedures related to engagement performance. In addition, policies and procedures related to the monitoring element of quality control enable a firm to evaluate whether its policies and procedures for each of the other five elements of quality control are suitably designed and effectively applied.

1.06 Policies and procedures established by the firm related to each element are designed to achieve reasonable assurance with respect to the purpose of that element. Deficiencies in policies and procedures for an element may result in not achieving reasonable assurance with respect to the purpose of that element; however, the system of quality control, as a whole, may still be effective in providing the firm with reasonable assurance that the firm and its personnel comply with professional standards and applicable regulatory and legal requirements and that the firm or engagement partners issue reports that are appropriate in the circumstances.

1.07 If a firm merges, acquires, sells, or otherwise changes a portion of its practice, the surviving firm evaluates and, as necessary, revises, implements, and maintains firm-wide quality control policies and procedures that are appropriate for the changed circumstances.

Leadership Responsibilities for Quality Within the Firm (the "Tone at the Top")

1.08 The purpose of the leadership responsibilities element of a system of quality control is to promote an internal culture based on the recognition that quality is essential in performing engagements. The firm should establish and maintain the following policies and procedures to achieve this purpose:

- Require the firm's leadership (managing partner, board of managing partners, CEO, or equivalent) to assume ultimate responsibility for the firm's system of quality control.
- Provide the firm with reasonable assurance that personnel assigned operational responsibility for the firm's quality control system have sufficient and appropriate experience and ability to identify and understand quality control issues and develop appropriate policies and procedures, as well as the necessary authority to implement those policies and procedures.

1.09 Establishing and maintaining the following policies and procedures assists firms in recognizing that the firm's business strategy is subject to the overarching requirement for the firm to achieve the objectives of the system of quality control in all the engagements that the firm performs:

- Assign management responsibilities so that commercial considerations do not override the quality of the work performed.
- Design policies and procedures addressing performance evaluation, compensation, and advancement (including incentive systems) with regard to personnel to demonstrate the firm's overarching commitment to the objectives of the system of quality control.
- Devote sufficient and appropriate resources for the development, communication, and support of its quality control policies and procedures.

Relevant Ethical Requirements

1.10 The purpose of the relevant ethical requirements element of a system of quality control is to provide the firm with reasonable assurance that the firm and its personnel comply with relevant ethical requirements when discharging professional responsibilities. Relevant ethical requirements include independence, integrity, and objectivity. Establishing and maintaining policies such as the following assist the firm in obtaining this assurance:

- Require that personnel adhere to relevant ethical requirements such as those in regulations, interpretations, and rules of the AICPA, state CPA societies, state boards of accountancy, state statutes, the U.S. Government Accountability Office, and any other applicable regulators.
- Establish procedures to communicate independence requirements to firm personnel and, where applicable, others subject to them.
- Establish procedures to identify and evaluate possible threats to independence and objectivity, including the familiarity threat that may be created by using the same senior personnel on an audit or attest engagement over a long period of time, and to take appropriate action to eliminate those threats or reduce them to an acceptable level by applying safeguards.
- Require that the firm withdraw from the engagement if effective safeguards to reduce threats to independence to an acceptable level cannot be applied.

- Require written confirmation, at least annually, of compliance with the firm's policies and procedures on independence from all firm personnel required to be independent by relevant requirements.
- Establish procedures for confirming the independence of another firm or firm personnel in associated member firms who perform part of the engagement. This would apply to national firm personnel, foreign firm personnel, and foreign-associated firms.[2]
- Require the rotation of personnel for audit or attest engagements where regulatory or other authorities require such rotation after a specified period.

Acceptance and Continuance of Client Relationships and Specific Engagements

1.11 The purpose of the quality control element that addresses acceptance and continuance of client relationships and specific engagements is to establish criteria for deciding whether to accept or continue a client relationship and whether to perform a specific engagement for a client. A firm's client acceptance and continuance policies represent a key element in mitigating litigation and business risk. Accordingly, it is important that a firm be aware that the integrity and reputation of a client's management could reflect the reliability of the client's accounting records and financial representations and, therefore, affect the firm's reputation or involvement in litigation. A firm's policies and procedures related to the acceptance and continuance of client relationships and specific engagements should provide the firm with reasonable assurance that it will undertake or continue relationships and engagements only where it

- is competent to perform the engagement and has the capabilities, including the time and resources, to do so;
- can comply with legal and relevant ethical requirements;
- has considered the client's integrity and does not have information that would lead it to conclude that the client lacks integrity; and
- has reached an understanding with the client regarding the services to be performed.

1.12 This assurance should be obtained before accepting an engagement with a new client, when deciding whether to continue an existing engagement, and when considering acceptance of a new engagement with an existing client. Establishing and maintaining policies such as the following assist the firm in obtaining this assurance:

- Evaluate factors that have a bearing on management's integrity and consider the risk associated with providing professional services in particular circumstances.[3]

---

[2] A *foreign-associated firm* is a firm domiciled outside of the United States and its territories that is a member of, correspondent with, or similarly associated with an international firm or international association of firms.

[3] Such considerations would include the risk of providing professional services to significant clients or to other clients for which the practitioner's objectivity or the appearance of independence

(continued)

Overview of Statements on Quality Control Standards

- Evaluate whether the engagement can be completed with professional competence; undertake only those engagements for which the firm has the capabilities, resources, and professional competence to complete; and evaluate, at the end of specific periods or upon occurrence of certain events, whether the relationship should be continued.

- Obtain an understanding, preferably in writing, with the client regarding the services to be performed.

- Establish procedures on continuing an engagement and the client relationship, including procedures for dealing with information that would have caused the firm to decline an engagement if the information had been available earlier.

- Require documentation of how issues relating to acceptance or continuance of client relationships and specific engagements were resolved.

Human Resources

1.13 The purpose of the human resources element of a system of quality control is to provide the firm with reasonable assurance that it has sufficient personnel with the capabilities, competence, and commitment to ethical principles necessary (*a*) to perform its engagements in accordance with professional standards and regulatory and legal requirements, and (*b*) to enable the firm to issue reports that are appropriate in the circumstances. Establishing and maintaining policies such as the following assist the firm in obtaining this assurance:

- Recruit and hire personnel of integrity who possess the characteristics that enable them to perform competently.

- Determine capabilities and competencies required for an engagement, especially for the engagement partner, based on the characteristics of the particular client, industry, and kind of service being performed. Specific competencies necessary for an engagement partner are discussed in paragraph .A27 of QC section 10.

- Determine the capabilities and competencies possessed by personnel.

- Assign the responsibility for each engagement to an engagement partner.

- Assign personnel based on the knowledge, skills, and abilities required in the circumstances and the nature and extent of supervision needed.

(footnote continued)

may be impaired. In broad terms, the significance of a client to a member or a firm refers to relationships that could diminish a practitioner's objectivity and independence in performing attest services. Examples of factors to consider in determining the significance of a client to an engagement partner, office, or practice unit include (*a*) the amount of time the partner, office, or practice unit devotes to the engagement, (*b*) the effect on the partner's stature within the firm as a result of his or her service to the client, (*c*) the manner in which the partner, office, or practice unit is compensated, or (*d*) the effect that losing the client would have on the partner, office, or practice unit.

©2017, AICPA

- Have personnel participate in general and industry-specific continuing professional education and professional development activities that enable them to accomplish assigned responsibilities and satisfy applicable continuing professional education requirements of the AICPA, state boards of accountancy, and other regulators.
- Select for advancement only those individuals who have the qualifications necessary to fulfill the responsibilities they will be called on to assume.

Engagement Performance

1.14 The purpose of the engagement performance element of quality control is to provide the firm with reasonable assurance (*a*) that engagements are consistently performed in accordance with applicable professional standards and regulatory and legal requirements, and (*b*) that the firm or the engagement partner issues reports that are appropriate in the circumstances. Policies and procedures for engagement performance should address all phases of the design and execution of the engagement, including engagement performance, supervision responsibilities, and review responsibilities. Policies and procedures also should require that consultation takes place when appropriate. In addition, a policy should establish criteria against which all engagements are to be evaluated to determine whether an engagement quality control review should be performed.

1.15 Establishing and maintaining policies such as the following assist the firm in obtaining the assurance required relating to the engagement performance element of quality control:

- Plan all engagements to meet professional, regulatory, and the firm's requirements.
- Perform work and issue reports and other communications that meet professional, regulatory, and the firm's requirements.
- Require that work performed by other team members be reviewed by qualified engagement team members, which may include the engagement partner, on a timely basis.
- Require the engagement team to complete the assembly of final engagement files on a timely basis.
- Establish procedures to maintain the confidentiality, safe custody, integrity, accessibility, and retrievability of engagement documentation.
- Require the retention of engagement documentation for a period of time sufficient to meet the needs of the firm, professional standards, laws, and regulations.
- Require that
    — consultation take place when appropriate (for example, when dealing with complex, unusual, unfamiliar, difficult, or contentious issues);
    — sufficient and appropriate resources be available to enable appropriate consultation to take place;

- all the relevant facts known to the engagement team be provided to those consulted;
- the nature, scope, and conclusions of such consultations be documented; and
- the conclusions resulting from such consultations be implemented.

• Require that
  - differences of opinion be dealt with and resolved;
  - conclusions reached are documented and implemented; and
  - the report not be released until the matter is resolved.

• Require that
  - all engagements be evaluated against the criteria for determining whether an engagement quality control review should be performed;
  - an engagement quality control review be performed for all engagements that meet the criteria; and
  - the review be completed before the report is released.

• Establish procedures addressing the nature, timing, extent, and documentation of the engagement quality control review.
• Establish criteria for the eligibility of engagement quality control reviewers.

Monitoring

1.16 The purpose of the monitoring element of a system of quality control is to provide the firm and its engagement partners with reasonable assurance that the policies and procedures related to the system of quality control are relevant, adequate, operating effectively, and complied with in practice. Monitoring involves an ongoing consideration and evaluation of the appropriateness of the design, the effectiveness of the operation of a firm's quality control system, and a firm's compliance with its quality control policies and procedures. The purpose of monitoring compliance with quality control policies and procedures is to provide an evaluation of the following:

• Adherence to professional standards and regulatory and legal requirements
• Whether the quality control system has been appropriately designed and effectively implemented
• Whether the firm's quality control policies and procedures have been operating effectively so that reports issued by the firm are appropriate in the circumstances

1.17 Establishing and maintaining policies such as the following assist the firm in obtaining the assurance required relating to the monitoring element of quality control:

- Assign responsibility for the monitoring process to a partner or partners or other persons with sufficient and appropriate experience and authority in the firm to assume that responsibility.
- Assign performance of the monitoring process to competent individuals.
- Require the performance of monitoring procedures that are sufficiently comprehensive to enable the firm to assess compliance with all applicable professional standards and the firm's quality control policies and procedures. Monitoring procedures consist of the following:
    — Review of selected administrative and personnel records pertaining to the quality control elements.
    — Review of engagement documentation, reports, and clients' financial statements.
    — Summarization of the findings from the monitoring procedures, at least annually, and consideration of the systemic causes of findings that indicate that improvements are needed.
    — Determination of any corrective actions to be taken or improvements to be made with respect to the specific engagements reviewed or the firm's quality control policies and procedures.
    — Communication of the identified findings to appropriate firm management personnel.
    — Consideration of findings by appropriate firm management personnel who should also determine that any actions necessary, including necessary modifications to the quality control system, are taken on a timely basis.
    — Assessment of
        - the appropriateness of the firm's guidance materials and any practice aids;
        - new developments in professional standards and regulatory and legal requirements and how they are reflected in the firm's policies and procedures where appropriate;
        - compliance with policies and procedures on independence;
        - the effectiveness of continuing professional development, including training;
        - decisions related to acceptance and continuance of client relationships and specific engagements; and
        - firm personnel's understanding of the firm's quality control policies and procedures and implementation thereof.
- Communicate at least annually, to relevant engagement partners and other appropriate personnel, deficiencies noted as a result of

Overview of Statements on Quality Control Standards

the monitoring process and recommendations for appropriate remedial action.
- Communicate the results of the monitoring of its quality control system process to relevant firm personnel at least annually.
- Establish procedures designed to provide the firm with reasonable assurance that it deals appropriately with the following:
  — Complaints and allegations that the work performed by the firm fails to comply with professional standards and regulatory and legal requirements.
  — Allegations of noncompliance with the firm's system of quality control.
  — Deficiencies in the design or operation of the firm's quality control policies and procedures, or noncompliance with the firm's system of quality control by an individual or individuals, as identified during the investigations into complaints and allegations.

  This includes establishing clearly defined channels for firm personnel to raise any concerns in a manner that enables them to come forward without fear of reprisal and documenting complaints and allegations and the responses to them.
- Require appropriate documentation to provide evidence of the operation of each element of its system of quality control. The form and content of documentation evidencing the operation of each of the elements of the system of quality control is a matter of judgment and depends on a number of factors, including the following, for example:
  — The size of the firm and the number of offices.
  — The nature and complexity of the firm's practice and organization.
- Require retention of documentation providing evidence of the operation of the system of quality control for a period of time sufficient to permit those performing monitoring procedures and peer review to evaluate the firm's compliance with its system of quality control, or for a longer period if required by law or regulation.

1.18 Some of the monitoring procedures discussed in the previous list may be accomplished through the performance of the following:
- Engagement quality control review
- Review of engagement documentation, reports, and clients' financial statements for selected engagements after the report release date
- Inspection[4] procedures

---

[4] *Inspection* is a retrospective evaluation of the adequacy of the firm's quality control policies and procedures, its personnel's understanding of those policies and procedures, and the extent of the firm's compliance with them. Although monitoring procedures are meant to be ongoing, they may include inspection procedures performed at a fixed point in time. Monitoring is a broad concept; inspection is one specific type of monitoring procedure.

Documentation of Quality Control Policies and Procedures

1.19 The firm should document each element of its system of quality control. The extent of the documentation will depend on the size, structure, and nature of the firm's practice. Documentation may be as simple as a checklist of the firm's policies and procedures or as extensive as practice manuals.

Glossary

This glossary summarizes definitions of the terms related to sustainability information used in this guide. It does not contain definitions of common attestation terms. Related terms are shown in parentheses. Terms used in a definition that are also defined in this glossary appear in bold font.

accuracy (of measurement). The closeness of agreement between a measured value and the actual value.

additionality. A project is *additional* if it would not have happened but for the incentive provided by the credit trading program (for example, Clean Development Mechanism [CDM] or Joint Implementation [JI]). The Kyoto Protocol specifies that only projects that provide GHG emission reductions that are *additional* to any that would occur in the absence of the project activity shall be awarded certified emission reductions (CERs) in the case of CDM projects, or emission reduction units (ERUs) in the case of JI projects. This is often referred to as *environmental additionality*. *Financial additionality* is the notion that a project is made commercially viable through its ability to generate value in the form of certified emission reductions. Various greenhouse gas (GHG) registries or regulatory frameworks may define these terms differently.

allowance. The unit of trade under a trading system. In a **closed trading system**, trading of allowances is permitted only between parties subject to the program or regulatory system. Allowances grant the holder the right to emit a specific quantity (for example, one ton) of GHG emissions once. The total quantity of allowances issued by regulators dictates the total quantity of GHG emissions possible under the system. Allowances are typically granted to emitters by governmental entities or agencies either for free or for a fee. At the end of each compliance period, each source must surrender sufficient allowances to cover its GHG emissions during that period. In an **open trading system**, trades can be made between parties within the system and parties outside the system.

baseline. A hypothetical scenario for what GHG emissions, removals, or storage would have been in the absence of the GHG project or project activity.[1]

base year. A specific historical year or an average over multiple historical years against which an entity's sustainability information (such as GHG emissions) is compared over time.

boundaries. There are three types of boundaries: **operational, organizational,** and **reporting**.

- **operational boundary.** Activities, including actions of third parties as a consequence of their interaction with the entity, that affect the entity's sustainability performance; an entity may recognize that its sustainability impacts and concerns extend beyond its organizational boundary; for example, GHG emissions of

---

[1] *The Greenhouse Gas Protocol—A Corporate Accounting and Reporting Standard* (revised edition) (WRI/WBCSD, 2004).

vendors (such as airlines and utility companies) as a consequence of doing business with the entity.

- **organizational boundary.** The legal composition of an entity for which it has direct or operational control over the entity's activities; common approaches used for organizational boundaries include equity share, financial control, and operational control.
- **reporting boundary.** The boundary used by the entity to report its **sustainability information**; it may include direct and indirect effects, including sustainability consequences of third parties that are within the entity's operational boundary. The reporting boundary, which is set by management for the sustainability information that is the subject of the engagement, may be for the subject matter of the entire entity, a portion of the entity, or certain sustainability indicators and may include the operational boundary for such subject matter.

Certain frameworks or standards may specify the boundaries to be used for purposes of reporting under such framework or standard. The World Resources Institute/World Business Council for Sustainable Development (WRI/WBCSD) Greenhouse Gas Protocol provides additional guidance on setting organizational and operational boundaries with respect to GHG emissions.

closed trading system. In a closed trading system, trading of **allowance**s is permitted only between parties subject to the program or regulatory system. See also **open trading system**.

credit. The term *credit* is used in a number of contexts, most commonly in relation to emission reductions that have been achieved in excess of the required amount for one of the following:

- The Kyoto Protocol's JI, also known as ERUs
- The Kyoto Protocol's CDM, specifically known as CERs
- The Kyoto-related and voluntary trading programs

direct GHG emissions. Direct GHG emissions, or Scope 1 emissions, are GHG emissions from sources that are owned or controlled by the entity. These are GHG emissions associated with the following:

- Stationary combustion from fuel burned in the entity's stationary equipment, such as boilers, incinerators, engines, and flares
- Mobile combustion from fuel burned in the entity's transport devices, such as trucks, trains, airplanes, and boats
- Process GHG emissions from physical or chemical processes, such as cement manufacturing, petrochemical processing, and aluminum smelting
- Fugitive GHG emissions, which include both intentional and unintentional releases, such as equipment leaks from joints and seals and GHG emissions from wastewater treatment, pits, and cooling towers

GHG emissions factor. A mathematical factor or ratio for converting the measure of an activity (for example, liters of fuel consumed, kilometers traveled, the number of animals in husbandry, or tons of product produced) into an estimate of the quantity of GHGs associated with that activity.

GHG emission reduction. The process by which an entity reduces its emissions of GHGs as compared to a **baseline**.

GHG emissions inventory. An entity's GHG emissions for a specified period, typically a year or a series of years, is referred to as its GHG emissions inventory. See also **baseline** and **base year**.

GHG emissions trading programs. There are two types of GHG emissions trading programs: **baseline-and-credit program**s and **cap-and-trade programs**.

- **baseline-and-credit program.** In a baseline-and-credit program (that is, credit- or project-based trading), each participant is provided a baseline against which its performance is measured. If an action is taken to reduce GHG emissions, the difference between the baseline and the actual GHG emissions, where actual GHG emissions are less than the baseline, can be credited and traded. The baseline established for crediting purposes can be fixed or dynamic, decreasing or increasing over time. The key distinction between a cap-and-trade program and a baseline-and-credit program is that under a cap-and-trade program, the regulated sources' GHG emissions are required to remain under a GHG emissions cap, which is a fixed quantity. Such a limit is not necessarily imposed in a baseline-and-credit program. The Kyoto Protocol's CDM, for example, would operate as a baseline-and-credit program.[2]

- **cap-and-trade program.** In a cap-and-trade program (that is, allowance-based trading), the maximum level of GHG emissions that can be released from sources is set by the control authority. This level is the cap, which the control authority may reduce over time. All sources are required to have **allowance**s to emit. The allowances are freely transferable; they can be bought or sold. The control authority issues exactly the number of allowances needed to produce the desired emission level. An example of this kind of system is the California Air Resources Board statewide Cap-and-Trade Program, under which allowances of CO2e can be traded to comply with a GHG emissions cap.

indirect GHG emissions. Indirect GHG emissions are classified as either Scope 2 or Scope 3 emissions under the WRI/WBCSD Greenhouse Gas Protocol. Scope 2 GHG emissions represent GHG emissions from the generation of imported or purchased electricity, heat, or steam. Scope 3 emissions under the GHG Protocol include the following examples:

- Employee business travel
- Outsourced activities, contract manufacturing, and franchises
- Transportation by the vendor or contractor of, for example, materials, products, waste, and employees
- GHG emissions from product use and end of life
- Employee commuting
- Production of imported materials

---

[2] Adapted from Richard Rosenzweig and Josef Janssen, *The Emerging International Greenhouse Gas Market* (Arlington: Pew Center on Global Climate Change, 2002).

internal control over sustainability information. A process effected by management, and other personnel, to provide reasonable assurance regarding the achievement of the entity's objectives with regard to the reliability of sustainability reporting and the preparation of **sustainability information**.

inventory. See **GHG emissions inventory**.

leakage. Leakage occurs when a GHG emission reduction project causes GHG emissions to increase beyond the project's **boundaries**. Entities entering into a GHG emission reduction project typically must demonstrate that the GHG emission reduction will not cause GHG emissions to increase beyond the project's boundaries.

management's specialist. An individual or organization possessing expertise in a field other than accounting or auditing, whose work in that field is used by the entity to assist the entity in preparing its sustainability information.

measurement. The value or result of a process of counting, measuring, estimating, valuing, or aggregating data; complete disclosure of the results of a measurement includes information about the unit of measure and, if material, the measurement uncertainty.

measurement method. The manner in which a particular indicator is measured (for example, using a meter or indirectly measuring the subject matter via a surrogate activity that is correlated with the subject matter being measured, such as measuring miles flown which is correlated with GHG emissions of certain greenhouse gases).

measurement uncertainty. A characteristic of a reported value that describes the dispersion of quantities that could reasonably be attributed to the reported value due to an inherent lack of **accuracy** or lack of **precision** of the measurement process; measurement uncertainty includes estimation uncertainty. Measurement uncertainty may be estimated for a reported matter using statistical and nonstatistical means.

nonstatistically estimated measurement uncertainty. Uncertainties in the measured value introduced by factors, such as limitations of measurement equipment, calibration limitations, the use of assumptions, the selection of measurement methods, or the intent (intentional bias) of the measuring or reporting party, that are estimated by nonstatistical methods. These sources of uncertainty can be difficult to estimate because they arise from imperfections in the measurement process that are not susceptible to estimation using statistical methods.

offset. Offsets are created when a source makes voluntary, permanent GHG emission reductions that are in surplus to any required reductions. Entities that create offsets can trade them to other entities to cover growth or relocation. Regulators may be required to approve each trade. Regulators normally require a portion of the offsets to be retired to ensure an overall reduction in GHG emissions. Offsets are an open system (an open system is one in which trades can be made between parties within the system and parties outside the system). One offset is a GHG emission reduction that a pollution source has achieved in excess of permitted levels, or required reductions, or both. The excess amount is the credit and can be sold on the market.

Glossary

open trading system. In an open trading system, trades can be made between parties within the system and parties outside the system. See also **closed trading system**.

operational boundary. See **boundaries**.

organizational boundary. See **boundaries**.

permits. Certificates of operation that allow holders to operate a facility provided they do not exceed a specified rate (kilograms/tons per day). Permits are often designated as an upper limit. Because few systems operate at 100 percent of capacity at all times, actual GHG emissions, for example, are usually a fraction of the theoretical upper limit of allowed GHG emissions. However, as new permits become harder to obtain, existing operations are motivated to increase their level of operations under their existing permits (for example, by adding a second shift, thereby legally increasing the overall quantity of GHG emissions). **Allowances** are transferable, whereas the permit itself is attached to a specific installation or site.

point value. The amount selected by management for recognition or disclosure in the sustainability information.

precision (of measurement). The degree of consistency and agreement among independent measurements of a quantity under the same conditions.

reporting boundary. See **boundaries**.

Scope 1 emissions. See **direct GHG emissions**.

Scope 2 emissions. See **indirect GHG emissions**.

Scope 3 emissions. See **indirect GHG emissions**.

specified indicators. Population of the **sustainability indicators** for which the practitioner has been engaged to perform an examination or review engagement.

statistically estimated measurement uncertainty. Random variability in the measured value from one **measurement** to another due to the **accuracy** and **precision** limitations of the measurement device or methodology. Statistically estimated uncertainty is derived from samples of repeated measurements for which the outcomes can be evaluated statistically. The larger the sample of measurement outcomes, generally, the lower the statistically estimated uncertainty.

sustainability indicators. Quantitative (including metrics) and qualitative **sustainability information** that is used to measure and report an entity's performance; such indicators may be presented alone or as a component of other sustainability information (for example, as part of a **sustainability report**).

sustainability information. Information about sustainability matters (such as economic, environmental, social and governance performance); **sustainability metrics** and **sustainability indicators** are components of sustainability information. Sustainability information may be nonquantitative (narrative), historical, or forward-looking.

sustainability metrics. Quantitative performance measures related to sustainability matters. Such metrics are usually part of a **sustainability report**.

sustainability report. A report that conveys **sustainability information** about the entity's performance regarding sustainability matters; also referred to by other names, such as a corporate social responsibility (CSR) report or an environmental, social and governance (ESG) report.

validation (GHG emissions). The process used to ensure that a given project, if implemented, can achieve the projected reduction results. The entity may validate the feasibility of the design of a GHG emission reduction project internally, or the entity may engage an outside party (typically an engineering or a consulting firm) to perform the validation.

verification (GHG emissions). The objective and independent assessment of whether the reported **GHG emissions inventory** properly reflects the GHG impact of the entity in conformance with pre-established GHG accounting and reporting standards. Some registries define verification as the process used to ensure that a given participant's GHG emissions inventory (either the **base year** or the annual result) has met a minimum quality standard and complied with a specific registry's procedures and protocols for calculating and reporting GHG emissions.

Index of Pronouncements and Other Technical Guidance

A

Title	Paragraphs
AT-C Section	
105, *Concepts Common to all Attestation Engagements*	1.24, 1.31, 1.33, 1.39, 1.46, 1.51, 2.26, 3.86, 4.10, 5.07, 5.34
205, *Examination Engagements*	1.52, 1.57, 2.01, 2.16, 2.22, 2.29E, 2.33E, 2.45, 3.02E, 3.14E–.15E, 3.18E–.19E, 3.31E, 3.34E, 3.37E–.38E, 3.41E, 3.44E, 3.46E, 3.49E, 3.53E, 3.53R, 3.55, 3.57E, 3.58E, 3.66E, 3.78, 3.79, 3.81, 3.83, 3.86, 4.01, 4.02, 4.05, 4.08, 4.10, 4.15, 4.16, 4.19, 4.42, 5.36, 5.52, 5.54, Appendix C, Appendix D, Appendix F
210, *Review Engagements*	1.52, 1.57, 2.01, 2.16, 2.29R, 2.33R, 2.45, 3.02E, 3.05R, 3.14R, 3.15R, 3.18R, 3.20R, 3.25, 3.44R, 3.46R, 3.49R, 3.53R, 3.55, 3.57R, 3.66R, 3.78–.79, 3.81, 3.83, 3.86, 4.01–.02, 4.05, 4.08, 4.10, 4.16, 4.18–.19, 4.44–.45, 5.36, 5.52, 5.54, Appendix C, Appendix E, Appendix F

C

Title	Paragraphs
Code of Professional Conduct	
ET section 1.200.001, *Independence Rule*	1.45, 4.35

P

Title	Paragraphs
Practice Aid *Establishing and Maintaining a System of Quality Control for a CPA Firm's Accounting and Auditing Practice*	Appendix G

Q

Title	Paragraphs
QC Section 10, *A Firm's System of Quality Control*	Appendix G

Subject Index

A

ACCOUNTANT'S REPORT. *See* **practitioner's report**

ADDITIONALITY, ENVIRONMENTAL 5.16

ADEQUACY OF DISCLOSURES
- Evaluating .... 3.70E, 3.70R, 3.71, 3.74E, ... 3.74R, 3.85, 5.54
- GHG emissions engagement 5.54
- Reporting considerations 4.02–.09, 4.48

ADVERSE OPINION 4.42

AGREEING ON TERMS OF ENGAGEMENT 1.52–.56

ANALYTICAL PROCEDURES
- Examination engagement .... 3.06E, ... 3.18–.19E, 3.24–.26
- GHG emissions engagement 5.44
- Review engagement .... 3.05R, 3.06R, ... 3.18–.19R, 3.24–.26

APPROPRIATENESS OF SUBJECT MATTER, ASSESSING ... 1.07, 1.27–.32, 5.22–.24

ASSERTIONS. *See* **written assertion**

ATTRIBUTES TO BE MET BY GHG EMISSION REDUCTIONS 5.15

B

BASE YEAR INFORMATION
- Generally 1.13
- GHG emissions 5.12

BASELINE FOR GHG EMISSIONS 5.10, 5.15

BOUNDARIES IN SUSTAINABILITY REPORTING
- Generally .... 1.08–.12, Figure 1-1 to 1-2 .... at 1.11
- GHG emissions 5.09–.11
- Planning considerations 2.14–.15
- Responding to assessed risks and obtaining evidence 3.17E, 3.17R
- Reporting considerations .... 4.04, 4.23, ... 4.36–.38

C

CDP (FORMERLY CARBON DISCLOSURE PROJECT) 5.05

CLIMATE REGISTRY 5.05

COMPARATIVE INFORMATION
- Forming an opinion or conclusion 4.04
- GHG emissions engagement 5.61
- Planning considerations 2.21
- Practitioner's reports 4.39–.41

CONCLUSION. *See also* **practitioner's report** 4.01–.09, 4.29, 4.44–.45

CONSISTENCY
- Examination engagement procedures 3.68–.70E, 3.71–.73
- GHG emissions information 5.39
- Planning considerations 2.20
- Review engagement procedures 3.68–.70R, 3.71–.73

CONTROLS. *See* **internal control**

CORRECTION OF MATERIAL MISSTATEMENT IN PREVIOUSLY ISSUED SUSTAINABILITY INFORMATION 4.46–.49

CORROBORATION, GHG EMISSIONS ENGAGEMENT 5.47

CREDIBLE GHG EMISSIONS BASELINE 5.15

CRITERIA
- Assessing availability 1.39–.40
- Assessing suitability 1.33–.38, 5.25–.26
- Description of 3.83–.85
- Measurement uncertainty 4.06
- Reporting considerations 4.14, 4.36–.38

D

DIAGRAMS OR GRAPHS IN SUSTAINABILITY INFORMATION .... 2.05, Appendix B

DESCRIPTION OF CRITERIA 3.83–.85

DIRECT GHG EMISSIONS 5.08

DISCLAIMER OF CONCLUSION 4.12

DISCLAIMER OF OPINION 4.12, 4.15

DOCUMENTATION 3.86, 5.57

E

ECONOMIC SUBJECT MATTER IN SUSTAINABILITY INFORMATION .... 1.05, ... 2.19

ELECTRICITY INDIRECT GHG EMISSIONS 5.08

ENGAGEMENT ACCEPTANCE, OTHER CONSIDERATIONS. *See also* **preconditions for engagement acceptance** 5.36

ENGAGEMENT LETTERS .... 1.39, ... 1.52–.54

ENVIRONMENTAL SUBJECT MATTER IN SUSTAINABILITY INFORMATION .... 1.05, ... 2.19

EVALUATING RESULTS OF PROCEDURES .... 3.57–.58E, 3.57R, ... 3.59–.65, 3.66E–.66R, 3.67, ... 3.68–.70E, 3.68–.70R, 3.71–.73, ... 3.74–.75E, 3.74–.75R, 3.76–.77

EVIDENCE
- Assessing ability to obtain 1.41–.44, 5.27
- Materiality considerations .... 2.33E, ... 2.33R, 2.34–.44
- Procedures to obtain .... 3.18–.23E, ... 3.18–.22R, 3.24–.30, 3.31–.43E, ... 3.31R, 3.34–.35R, 3.39–.40R
- Responding to assessed risks and obtaining .... 3.14–.15E, 3.14–.15R, ... 3.16, 3.17E, 3.17R
- Revision of risk assessment .... 3.46–.48E, ... 3.46R
- Sufficiency and appropriateness of 4.01–.09, 4.15, 4.18

EXAMINATION REPORT. *See* **practitioner's report**

EXTERNAL SPECIALIST, USE OF. *See* **practitioner's specialist, using work of**

F

FACTUAL NARRATIVE IN SUSTAINABILITY INFORMATION ...2.05, 2.08, Appendix B

FRAUD, LAWS, AND REGULATIONS ...3.44E, ... 3.44R, 3.45, 5.44

FURTHER PROCEDURES 3.18–.23E

G

GHG EMISSIONS. *See* **greenhouse gas (GHG) emissions engagements, supplemental guidance**

GOVERNANCE SUBJECT MATTER IN SUSTAINABILITY INFORMATION ....1.05, ... 2.19

GREENHOUSE GAS (GHG) EMISSIONS ENGAGEMENTS, SUPPLEMENTAL GUIDANCE 5.01–.61
- Adequacy of disclosure, evaluating or considering 5.54
- Appropriateness of subject matter, assessing 5.22–.24
- Base year 5.12, 5.44E, 5.44R, 5.50, 5.61
- Boundaries for 5.09–.11
- Calculation techniques .... 5.44E, 5.44R, ... 5.48–.50
- Comparative information 5.61
- Documentation 5.57
- Engagement acceptance, other considerations 5.36
- Evidence, assessing ability to obtain 5.27
- Generally 5.01–.17
- Illustrative procedures 5.42–.54
- Independence 5.28

GREENHOUSE GAS (GHG) EMISSIONS ENGAGEMENTS, SUPPLEMENTAL GUIDANCE—continued
- Inventory 5.53
- Matters of emphasis 5.60
- Measurement uncertainty 5.17
- Objectives of examination engagement 5.18–.19
- Objectives of review engagement ... 5.20–.21
- Other information 5.56
- Other practitioner, using work of ....5.33–.35, ... 5.58
- Planning the engagement 5.38–.39
- Potential misstatements 5.40
- Practitioner's specialist, using work of ... 5.41
- Preconditions for engagement acceptance. *See also* engagement acceptance, other considerations 5.22–.32
- Professional competence considerations 5.29–.32
- Reduction projects 5.13–.16
- Reporting considerations 5.58–.61
- Significant inherent limitations 5.59
- Subsequent events 5.52
- Suitability of criteria, assessing 5.25–.26
- Written assertion, requesting 5.37
- Written representations ...5.44E, 5.44R, 5.55

GREENHOUSE GAS (GHG) EMISSIONS REDUCTION PROJECTS. *See also* **greenhouse gas (GHG) emissions engagements, supplemental guidance** 5.13–.16

GREENHOUSE GAS (GHG) EMISSIONS TRADING PROGRAM 5.04

I

INCREASED FOCUS IN AREAS OF INCREASED RISK, PLACING .... 3.02–.06R, 3.07, ... 3.09R, 3.10–.13, 5.40

INDEPENDENCE 1.45, 4.35, 5.28

INDIRECT GHG EMISSIONS 5.08

INFORMATION SYSTEMS EXPERTISE ... 5.31

INQUIRIES
- Examination engagement 3.27–3.30
- Review engagement .... 3.20–.22R, ... 3.27–3.30, 3.39R, 5.42, 5.47

INTERNAL AUDITORS, USING WORK OF
- Examination procedures ... 3.21E, 3.53–.54E, ... 3.55, 5.44E
- GHG emissions engagement 5.44E, 5.44R
- Planning considerations 2.22
- Review procedures ...3.53–.54R, 3.55, 5.44R

INTERNAL CONTROL. *See also* **tests of controls**
- Operating effectiveness of controls .... 3.31E, ... 3.33E, 3.38E
- Planning considerations 2.17, 2.19

Subject Index

INTERNAL CONTROL—continued
- Risk assessment 2.29–.31E, 2.32
- Understanding in review engagement 2.29–.30R, 2.32, 3.31R

INVENTORY, GHG EMISSIONS 5.53

L

LAWS AND REGULATIONS, REPORTING ON GHG EMISSIONS FOR COMPLIANCE WITH. *See also* fraud, laws, and regulations 5.04

LEGAL LETTER, REQUESTING .... 3.21E, ... 3.22R, 5.44E

M

MANAGEMENT. *See also* responsible party
- Corroboration 5.47
- Discussion of misstatements with ...... 3.75E, ... 3.75R
- Material interpretations of criteria .... 4.14, ... 3.85
- Responsibilities ...... 1.52, 3.78, 4.15, 4.18, ... 4.22

MANAGEMENT-DEVELOPED CRITERIA, ASSESSING AVAILABILITY 1.39–.40

MANAGEMENT'S SPECIALIST, USING WORK OF 3.51E

MATERIAL CHANGE IN CRITERIA, MEASUREMENT METHOD, OR REPORTING BOUNDARY, PRACTITIONER'S REPORT 4.36–.38

MATERIAL MATTERS, CONSIDERING ADEQUACY OF DISCLOSURE 4.02–.09, 5.54

MATERIALITY IN PLANNING AND PERFORMING THE ENGAGEMENT .... 2.03, 2.07, 2.33E, ... 2.33R, 2.34–.44

MATTERS OF EMPHASIS IN PRACTITIONER'S REPORT 4.35, 5.60

MEASUREMENT METHODS
- Consistency in GHG emissions 5.39
- Effect of changes in accepting engagement 1.44
- Generally 1.14, 1.16
- Reporting considerations .... 4.03, 4.23, ... 4.36–.38
- Suitability of criteria assessment 1.35–.37

MEASUREMENT UNCERTAINTY
- Defined 1.15
- Forming an opinion or conclusion ... 4.06–.09
- Generally 1.14–.21
- GHG emissions 5.17
- Illustrative examples .... Appendix A
- Materiality consideration 2.36–.37

MEASUREMENT UNCERTAINTY—continued
- Planning considerations 2.23–.24
- Procedures 3.37–.40E, 3.39–.40R
- Risks of material misstatement, identifying .... 3.07, 3.08–.09E, 3.09R, ... 3.10–.13
- Significant inherent limitations 4.33

MISSTATEMENTS
- Evaluating 3.57R, 3.57–.58E, 3.59–.64
- GHG emissions information 5.40
- In previously issued sustainability information .... 3.74–.75E, 3.74–.75R, ... 3.76–.77
- Revision of risk assessment due to .... 3.46R, ... 3.46–.48E
- Types associated with sustainability information 2.41

MODIFIED CONCLUSION 4.44–.45
MODIFIED OPINION 4.29, 4.42–.43

N

NARRATIVE STATEMENTS ON SUSTAINABILITY INFORMATION .... 2.05, ... 2.08, Appendix B

NONCOMPLIANCE WITH LAWS AND REGULATIONS. *See* fraud, laws, and regulations

O

OBJECTIVES, OF
- Examination of sustainability information 1.22
- Examination of GHG emissions information 5.18
- Examination of GHG emission reduction information 5.19
- Review of sustainability information 1.23
- Review of GHG emissions information 5.20
- Review of GHG emission reduction information 5.21

OPERATING EFFECTIVENESS OF CONTROLS, EVALUATING. *See also* internal control and tests of controls .... 2.17, 3.33E, ... 3.38E

OPERATIONAL BOUNDARY. *See* boundaries in sustainability reporting

OPINION. *See also* practitioner's report 4.01–.09, 4.42–.43

ORGANIZATIONAL BOUNDARY. *See* boundaries in sustainability reporting

OTHER INFORMATION
- GHG emissions 5.56
- Performing procedures 3.81–.82

OTHER PRACTITIONER, USING WORK OF
- Generally 1.51
- GHG emissions 5.33–.35, 5.58

©2017, AICPA

AAG-SUST OTH

OTHER PRACTITIONER, USING WORK OF—continued
- Performing procedures 3.56
- Planning considerations 2.25–.27
- Practitioner's reports .... 4.24–.30, ... Appendix D, Appendix E

OTHER REVIEW PROCEDURES 3.34–.35R

P

PARTY REQUESTING ENGAGEMENT, ASSESSING ABILITY TO OBTAIN EVIDENCE. *See also* **responsible party** 1.41

PERFORMING EXAMINATION OR REVIEW PROCEDURES 3.01–.86, 5.40–.57

PLANNING CONSIDERATIONS 2.01–.27
- Boundaries 2.14–.15
- Collection and reporting process characteristics 2.16–.19
- Comparative information 2.21
- Consistency 2.20
- Generally 2.01–.02
- GHG emissions information 5.38–.39
- Internal audit 2.22
- Measurement uncertainty 2.23–.24
- Nature and characteristics of subject matter 2.03–.10
- Organization structure and nature of business 2.11–.13
- Other practitioner, using work of 2.25–.27

PLANNING THE ENGAGEMENT. *See also* **planning considerations** 2.01–.45
- Planning considerations 2.01–.27
- GHG emissions information 5.38–.39
- Materiality .... 2.03, 2.07, 2.33E, 2.33R, ... 2.34–.44
- Risk assessment procedures .... 2.28, ... 2.29–.30R, 2.29–.31R, 2.32
- Practitioner's specialist, using work of ... 2.45

PRACTITIONER'S REPORT 4.01–.49, 5.58–.61
- Comparative information 4.39–.41, 5.61
- Content 4.15–.41
- Correction of material misstatement in previously issued sustainability information 4.46–.49
- Examination of one or more specified indicators and review of others, illustrative report .... Appendix F
- Examination report, illustrative examples .... Appendix D
- Forming an opinion or conclusion ... 4.01–.09
- Review report, illustrative examples .... Appendix E
- Agreeing on terms of engagement 1.56
- Material change in criteria, measurement method, or reporting boundary 4.36–.38
- Matters of emphasis 4.35, 5.60

PRACTITIONER'S REPORT—continued
- Modified conclusions ... 4.29, 4.44–.45, 5.61
- Modified opinions 4.42–.43, 5.61
- Other practitioner, references to report of .... 1.51, 4.24–.30, 5.58, Appendix D, ... Appendix E
- Preparing 4.10–.14
- Significant inherent limitations ...... 4.31–.34, ... 5.59

PRACTITIONER'S SPECIALIST, USING WORK OF
- Examination procedures 3.53–.54E, 3.55
- Considering use of 1.48–.50, 5.41
- GHG emissions engagement 5.41
- Considerations when selecting and using work of 2.45
- Review procedures 3.53–.54R, 3.55

PRECONDITIONS FOR ENGAGEMENT ACCEPTANCE 1.24–.50
- GHG emissions engagement 5.22–.32

PREDECESSOR PRACTITIONER .... 3.75–.77, ... 4.41, 4.49

PROCEDURES OTHER THAN TESTS OF CONTROL 3.34–.36E

PROFESSIONAL COMPETENCE CONSIDERATIONS ...1.46–.47, 5.29–.32

Q

QUALIFIED OPINION 4.42

QUALITY CONTROL STANDARDS, OVERVIEW .... Appendix G

QUANTIFIED SUSTAINABILITY INFORMATION .... 2.05, Appendix B

R

RELIABILITY OF INFORMATION PRODUCED BY ENTITY, EVALUATING
- Examination engagement 3.49–.52E
- Review engagement 3.49R

REPORTING. *See* **practitioner's report**

REPORTING BOUNDARY. *See* **boundaries in sustainability reporting**

REPORTING FRAMEWORK 1.07

REPRESENTATION LETTERS, ILLUSTRATIVE EXAMPLES. *See also* **written representations** .... Appendix C

RESPONDING TO ASSESSED RISKS AND OBTAINING EVIDENCE
- Examination engagement ... 3.14–.15E, 3.16, ... 3.17E
- Reporting boundary 3.17E, 3.17R
- Review engagement .... 3.14–.15R, 3.16, ... 3.17R

Subject Index

RESPONSIBLE PARTY. *See also* **management**
- Engaging party distinguished from 3.79
- Inquiries about the subject matter ... 3.27–.28
- Measurement uncertainty 4.09
- Subsequent events 3.66E, 3.66R
- Written assertion. *See also* management Appendix D, Appendix E .... 1.57–.58, 4.15, ... 4.17–.18, 4.20, 4.22, 5.37
- Written representations .... 3.75E, 3.75R, ... 3.78–.80, 5.44E, 5.44R, 5.55, ... Appendix C

RESULTS OF PROCEDURES, EVALUATING. *See* **evaluating results of procedures**

REVIEW REPORT. *See* **practitioner's report**

REVISION OF RISK ASSESSMENT
- Examination engagement 3.46–.48E
- Review engagement 3.46R

RISK ASSESSMENT PROCEDURES ..... 2.28, ... 2.29–.30R, 2.29–.31E, 2.32

RISKS OF MATERIAL MISSTATEMENT, IDENTIFYING .... 3.02–.06E, 3.07, ... 3.08–.09E, 3.10–.13, 5.40

S

SAMPLING, EXAMINATION ENGAGEMENT 3.41–.43E

SCIENTIFIC AND ENGINEERING EXPERTISE 5.31

SIGNIFICANT INHERENT LIMITATIONS ...... 4.15, 4.18, 4.31–.34, ... 5.59

SITE VISITS, GHG EMISSIONS ENGAGEMENT 5.45–.46

SOCIAL SUBJECT MATTER IN SUSTAINABILITY INFORMATION 1.05

SOFT NARRATIVE IN SUSTAINABILITY INFORMATION ... 2.05, 2.08, Appendix B

SPECIALISTS, USE OF. *See* **practitioner's specialist, use of and management's specialist, using work of**

SUBSEQUENT EVENTS AND SUBSEQUENTLY DISCOVERED FACTS ...... 3.66E, 3.66R, ... 3.67, 5.44, 5.52

SUITABILITY OF CRITERIA, ASSESSING 1.33–.38, 5.25–.26

SUSTAINABILITY INDICATORS 1.06

SUSTAINABILITY INFORMATION
- Characteristics of .... 2.05, Appendix B
- Generally 1.01–.07, 5.01

SUSTAINABILITY METRICS 1.06

T

TERMS OF ENGAGEMENT. *See* **agreeing on terms of engagement**

TESTS OF CONTROLS. *See also* **internal control** 3.23E, 3.31R, 3.31–.33E

THIRD PARTIES
- Assessing evidence availability 1.42
- Examination procedures 3.20E

U

UNIT OF MEASUREMENT, REPORTING ON CHANGE IN 4.37

V

VALIDATION, PROHIBITION ON USE OF IN PRACTITIONER'S REPORT 4.10

VALIDATION IN GHG EMISSIONS INFORMATION, DEFINED 5.06

VERIFICATION, PROHIBITION ON USE OF IN PRACTITIONER'S REPORT 4.10

VERIFICATION IN GHG EMISSIONS INFORMATION 5.06, 5.35

W

WITHDRAWING FROM ENGAGEMENTS 4.44–.45

WRITTEN ASSERTION
- Reporting considerations ... 4.15, 4.17, 4.18, ... 4.20, 4.22, Appendix D, and Appendix E
- Requesting 1.57–.58, 5.37

WRITTEN REPRESENTATIONS
- GHG emissions 5.44E, 5.44R, 5.55
- Illustrative representation letters ...Appendix C
- Performing procedures .... 3.75E, 3.75R, ... 3.78–.80

©2017, AICPA AAG-SUST WRI